After the Wildfire

John Alcock

AFTER THE WILDFIRE

Ten Years of Recovery
from the Willow Fire

THE UNIVERSITY OF
ARIZONA PRESS
TUCSON

The University of Arizona Press
www.uapress.arizona.edu

Printed in the United States of America

22   21   20   19   18   17   6   5   4   3   2   1

ISBN-13: 978-0-8165-3403-6 (paper)

Cover design by Leigh McDonald
Cover art from photos by John Alcock

All photographs are by the author unless otherwise noted.

Library of Congress Cataloging-in-Publication Data
Names: Alcock, John, 1942– author.
Title: After the wildfire : ten years of recovery from the Willow Fire / John Alcock.
Description: Tucson : The University of Arizona Press, 2017. | Includes bibliographical
    references and index.
Identifiers: LCCN 2016027502 | ISBN 9780816534036 (alk. paper)
Subjects: LCSH: Willow Fire, 2004. | Wildfires—Environmental aspects—Arizona—
    Mazatzal Mountains. | Fire ecology—Arizona—Mazatzal Mountains. | Mazatzal
    Mountains (Ariz.)—Environmental conditions—History—21st century.
Classification: LCC SD421.32.A7 A43 2017 | DDC 363.3709791—dc23 LC record available
    at https://lccn.loc.gov/2016027502

♾ This paper meets the requirements of ANSI/NISO Z39.48-1992 (Permanence of Paper).

Contents

After the Wildfire

Deer Creek Long Ago

In early September 1992, I went on an all-day hike, repeating one I had done some years previously. At the start, I walked upstream along the main branch of Deer Creek, which flows out of the Mazatzal Mountains in central Arizona. Eventually I left the creek, following a trail that climbed uphill through the forest for a considerable distance. When I finally reached a forest road on the far ridgetop, I went to my left for a short ways before dropping down on another long trail through the forest until I reached the south fork of the creek. From there, it was a major slog eastward and downward until I reached the trailhead again by State Route 87.

The first time I had followed this route, snow had fallen on the higher elevations of the Mazatzals, making it challenging to follow the trail in places. But I had persevered (nervously) and was rewarded by not getting lost or having to retrace my steps when far into the hike. Neither of these options had appealed to me. The mild anxiety I experienced then probably made the fifteen-mile trip seem longer than it was. As it was, completing the loop left me thoroughly tired. Today I am also weary at the end, but the excursion was straightforward. Free from concern about getting lost or reaching a dead end of some sort, I simply walked along, listening to the stream spilling over the rocks, while watching the big water bugs and whirligig beetles disporting themselves in the clear pools along the way. Both the main branch and the south fork were flowing nicely at the time, testimony to the decent monsoon season that was just drawing to a close.

In the midmorning, I found a comfortable rock in the shade by a large pool where I ate a banana and a brownie. In the middle of my "picnic," a large moth came fluttering in over the water to land on the rock wall on the other side of the creek. As the moth landed, it concealed its gaudy, bright orange and black hind wings done up in a migraine aura pattern; after landing, only its dark brown forewings were visible, as is typical for many moths in the genus *Catocala* (figure 1). I was aware that underwing moths are thought to expose their conspicuous hind wings in flight so that an attacking bird will grasp an expendable hind wing instead of grabbing the moth by its forewing and vital thorax or head. In addition, perched moths may flash their hind wings if pecked by a hungry bird that has discovered them; this action may startle the predator, inducing the attacker to abandon the prey or at the very least hesitate momentarily, during which time the moth may take off and escape.

These conclusions about the function of the beautiful hind wings were initially deduced largely from inspection of specimens with the kind of wing damage (V-shaped excisions) likely to have been caused by (disappointed) birds. Subsequently, experiments with captive blue jays exposed to artificial models of *Catocala* moths have confirmed that naïve birds are indeed startled when they encounter "prey" with brightly colored "wing" patterns similar to those of various species of underwing moths. Moreover, birds that have learned to associate one particular hind wing color pattern with the standard cryptic forewing pattern give every appearance of being surprised if they subsequently encounter another kind of colorful hind wing on a potential prey, a fact that may contribute to the great variety in *Catocala* hind wing colors and designs. The diversity of hind wing colors reflects the fact that there are well over one hundred species in the genus *Catocala* in North America alone.

The flying *Catocala* moth I watched near Deer Creek switched from being highly visible in flight to becoming highly inconspicuous once it had landed and ceased to move. However, the brief disturbance caused

Figure 1a. A *Catocala* underwing moth that has exposed its brilliantly colored hind wings. Photograph by Evan Rand.

Figure 1b. An Arizonan *Catocala* underwing moth resting with its hind wings concealed. Photograph by Elizabeth Makings.

by the moth as it came onto the rock caused another nearby moth of the same species to move slightly, revealing its existence in so doing. Had the already-perched moth stayed put, I would never have known it was there, thanks to its highly cryptic forewings. As I peered at the shady rock wall across the water, I then made out a third moth of this species plastered onto the rock wall, now that I was fully attuned to their appearance at rest. Perhaps the aggregation contained more than three moths, but if so, the others managed to remain hidden from view courtesy of their highly camouflaged forewings.

In the twenty years that have passed since my unexpected encounter with the three *Catocala* moths of Deer Creek, I have not seen them again. Indeed, one of the standard features of walking almost anywhere in natural places is unique natural history moments, which can surprise and entertain the walker. In the case of the *Catocala* moths, I am still puzzled that three individuals had somehow managed to come together on the same rock surface within a few feet of one another. Were two of the individuals males attracted to a receptive female? If so, why did the moths remain immobile after landing? Moreover, if, as I suppose, *Catocala* moths are active primarily at night, then why was the moth I observed flying around during the day? While I sat on the streamside rock, I pondered these matters for a while. Then, after polishing off my brownie, I resumed my hike, unaware that I was not going to see *Catocala* moths again here any time soon. Incidentally, I have subsequently learned that on the order of ten species of underwing moths may occur in and around the Mazatzals. So, the members of even this one genus of insects could surprise and delight me again on my walks in these mountains, if I am lucky.

During much of my long hike up and then down branches of Deer Creek on that distant day, I entertained myself by bird-watching. Even though the bird species of the area are familiar to me and so cannot match the *Catocala* moths in terms of novelty, I was not about to turn up my nose at the local songbirds, which were unusually numerous on that long-ago day. Part of the abundance of birds stemmed from an influx of migrants heading south, like the Townsend's and hermit warblers that I spotted. Many others bred here, especially in the high forests of ponderosa and pine where I added hepatic tanagers, painted redstarts, red-breasted nuthatches, and Steller's jays to my day list. When I imitated, as best I could, the simple whistled call of a pygmy owl (a predator of small birds), and then added *psshti*ng sounds (which imitate the mobbing calls of birds that have found a hawk or owl to harass), I was sometimes rewarded by the arrival of a confetti of real birds that added their genuine mobbing calls to the false signals I was producing. Flocks of bridled titmice hurried over to see what was up and then were joined by warblers, vireos, bushtits, and nuthatches, some of which landed very close by and peered down at me, evidently trying to determine where the unwanted predator was, perhaps the better to encourage it to move somewhere else.

Toward the end of my walk, I stopped calling in birds and concentrated merely on bringing the hike to a close. By midafternoon, I had made my way downhill to the south fork of Deer Creek. The trail here parallels the creek, which is narrower than its brother stream to the north. But in September 1992, both drainages were thickly lined with tall sycamores and hefty Emory oaks, the former smooth barked and more or less straight and tall, the latter with corrugated bark and twisted trunks.

One big sycamore of many provided perches for two large hawks that flapped up and then began to circle slowly over the stream as I approached. Black plumage, a tail with two white bands on black, and a pale base to the bill. The common black hawk, not at all common here and a wonderful coda to the bird-watching element of my hike. I did not know, nor did the common black hawks know, that in twelve years, a fierce wildfire would burn the streamside trees down to the ground as well as incinerate the hillside chaparral, destroying the nesting habitat of the hawks and the resources upon which they and many other birds depended. As it was, I was thrilled to see the big black hawks and to sense or at least to imagine a hint of fall along the stream where I saw flowering goldenrod, stands of poison ivy that were well past their prime, and the red fruit of the sugar sumacs. In retrospect, perhaps it was better for me not to know what was in store for Deer Creek and the mountains through which it flows in the summer of 2004.

The South Fork of
Deer Creek

January 2004

One of the reasons why I have been back to Deer Creek so many times over the years is that the trailhead is only a little over an hour's drive from my home in Tempe, Arizona, and just a short distance from State Route 87, whose four lanes are often loaded with traffic rushing north to Payson or back to Phoenix. In contrast, the parking area is never overburdened with vehicles or filled with hikers, even on weekends.

Another positive feature is that the trail begins at an elevation of about 3,300 feet, more than 2,000 feet higher than the suburb of Phoenix where I live, which means that it is always noticeably cooler up at the edge of the Mazatzal Mountains than it is back home. The relative coolness of the area is not a talking point in January, but during the heat of the year (which extends from May through September, or October, in and around Phoenix), I am grateful to lose a handful of degrees whenever I come up here from the Valley of the Sun.

The trail itself parallels the noisy highway for a short distance but soon provides three options that turn away from the road and head west into the quiet of the mountains. The first of three is Trail 47, the Gold Ridge Trail that runs toward the top of the mountain ridge to the west. I have taken this trail just once because I found it far too vertical to be enjoyable. The trail cuts through dense chaparral as it drives straight up the mountainside, forcing me on my only time there to pause and gasp for air often, my heart beating frantically.

The second is Trail 46, the South Fork Trail, which appropriately enough follows the south fork of Deer Creek as it climbs much more sedately, at least initially, into a canyon that cuts its way into the Mazatzals. This trail is my favorite of the three because it takes the walker away from the highway more promptly than the third trail, Trail 45, the Deer Creek Trail proper, which uses the main fork of Deer Creek as a passage into the mountains. Not only can I achieve blessed freedom from traffic noise more quickly on the South Fork Trail, I think most persons come here to use Trail 45, which means that the solitude quotient is usually greater along the southern branch. Or so I convince myself. Actually, neither trail is overrun with hikers at any time of the year, which makes either one well worth visiting.

Both trails (45 and 46) have the advantage of a less demanding ascent as well as sooner or later bringing the walker close to flowing water. For those of us who live in the desiccated heart of the Sonoran Desert, hikes that involve streams are particularly welcome. Today in the middle of winter, I will soon find that the above-ground component of the stream has come far down the south fork, having been recharged by winter rains and a little snowmelt from the higher reaches. To get to the creek itself, I walk along the trail as it crosses an open scruffy pasture that has been grazed on many occasions by a mob of hungry steers. The water in the south fork is cool and clear, not quite burbling as it moves over the gray and pink rocks that cover the bottom of the stream but definitely alive and well (figure 2). The edge of the stream is lined with sycamores and junipers and oaks, many of them substantial trees that contribute to the sensation of walking down a shaded tunnel in places where the trail stays close to the water. An autumn's worth of fallen brown sycamore leaves fills the gaps between boulders and stones, while other leaves lie completely submerged in water.

As the trail proceeds, the junipers grow closer together and clumps of pale brown grass accent the edge of the stream. The creek itself is usually no more than six feet wide and rarely more than a foot deep, but

Figure 2. Deer Creek before the Willow Fire when it was a sedate, wooded stream.

it moves downhill tranquilly in a shallow basin between the tree-lined stream banks. The barely rippled water surface acts as a mirror, reflecting the overarching limbs and trunks of the nearby oaks and junipers. A ladder-backed woodpecker flees from my approach. A wooden sign announces the start of the Mazatzal Wilderness, a tract intended to be free of motorized vehicles, which it is, thank goodness.

I could, if I wished, walk all the way up to the ridgeline some seven or so miles from the trailhead. This hike would take me past the scattered junipers low down and up and into a forest of taller pines and eventually to the higher elevations where thick-trunked ponderosas grow. I would come to Forest Road 201 at the very top, and then make my way down to the main fork of Deer Creek before heading back to the trailhead parking area, the reverse of the route I followed in September 1992. But I am older and so do not feel up to the challenge of a fifteen-mile round trip. After about three hours of climbing, I turn around and make my way back to my waiting vehicle, the return trip consuming only about two hours now that I am heading downhill.

An Internet site that describes the walk gives it a mere 2.5 stars out of 5. I, on the other hand, am more generous, as I find the flowing water, the white-barked sycamores lower down, the tall pines higher up, the silence of the mountain canyon, the occasional Townsend's solitaire and bridled titmouse, the alternating shade and sunshine on the stream, and all the other features of this relatively little-used trail extremely appealing. May the critical trail rater go elsewhere and lure other hikers away from Deer Creek. I need no company, only the stream, the sycamores, the steep hillsides, the forest birds, and the stark blue winter sky far overhead.

The Willow Fire and Its Aftermath

June 2004 and April 2005

On June 24, 2004, a lightning strike started a fire in the Mazatzal Mountains not far from the town of Payson, Arizona. The fire grew rapidly and eventually consumed nearly 200 square miles of forest and chaparral before running out of steam many days later in July (figure 3). During the time it was blazing, almost 1,000 firefighters joined battle to keep the fire out of Payson, a goal that was achieved. But by the time the intense Willow Fire was history, it had destroyed large parts of the unoccupied Mazatzals.

At the time it occurred, the Willow Fire was the third-largest wildfire in Arizona history, but since 2004, several others have superseded it. Indeed, of the ten largest fires ever recorded in our state, eight have flamed up in the last decade. These big, destructive fires were started by lightning, arson, stupidity, and the like, but they probably owed their eventual large size and ferocity to a combination of factors, such as the long history of fire suppression in some Arizona forests that enabled big fuel loads to accumulate, as well as drought and high temperatures, which dried out the forests and made them vulnerable to lightning and other fire starters. One double-barreled fire owed its beginnings to an arsonist in one place and a stranded motorist, who set a bonfire to catch the attention of potential rescuers, in another. The nonarsonist was

Figure 3. The Willow Fire in progress in the Mazatzal Mountains of central Arizona. Photograph by Eric Neitzel.

rescued by a helicopter, but the forest in which she had become lost was not saved. In fact, the two fires eventually joined up and created a monster inferno that for a time was on the verge of incinerating some of the mountain towns in northeastern Arizona.

Many of the recent big fires occurred during the very dry, very hot premonsoon, a time when many storms occur that produce no rain, only thunder and lightning. These conditions are perfect for fire ignition, and the Willow Fire was one such result. Whatever its cause, the wildfire drastically changed the landscape of the Mazatzals. These changes are what this book is all about because I have had the privilege of tracking what has happened to Deer Creek in the years since the Willow Fire, a task I began in April 2005 when I talked my wife, Sue, into coming with me on the drive up to Deer Creek so that we could see what the place looked like nine months or so after the event. Neither of us knew what to expect at our destination. But once we reached the creek, we found the effects of the fire were still very obvious and somewhat upsetting, indeed so much so that Sue decided that she did not want to walk the South Fork Trail again anytime soon. What we saw at the outset was a stream course that had been greatly widened by violent floods that had come down the drainage after the fire (figure 4).

Although on the day of our visit, only a thin ribbon of silvery water ran down the middle of what was now a broad and rocky creek, at other times, there must have been a torrent rampaging downstream from bank to bank. The Willow Fire had burnt the chaparral down to the ground and also destroyed the trees that once made the riparian zone of the creek proper a special place. When rains came, as they were sure to do eventually, the water rushed straight off the barren hillsides and into the now obstacle-free creek. Flash floods cut deeply into the creek bed while sweeping the adjacent banks clean. Sycamores that had once arched gracefully over the shallow stream were reduced to charcoal stumps buried under the rocks that the floodwaters pushed in front of them. A few dead sycamores still stood in the middle of the now greatly enlarged stream bed, but others had been completely uprooted and tossed downstream to lie in jumbles here and there. Junipers on the nearby hillside were blackened and leafless, some with long black strips of burnt bark dangling from dead trunks. Most still stood upright but without a hint of life except for a scattered handful of specimens that had somehow escaped the worst effects of the fire. These lucky trees sported a few limbs whose green juniper needles signaled that they had survived and were attempting a comeback.

Upstream, where the floods had cut channels into what had once been a shallow U-shaped basin that contained the old creek (figure 5), bare rock walls six feet high (or even higher) now rose straight up above what was a trickle of water today but had been anything but a trickle in the postfire past.

The grimness of the landscape was, however, softened considerably by the greenery that had sprung up on the ravaged hillsides. In fact, great stands of barley, the plants nearly two feet tall, covered much of the north-facing slope on one side of the creek (figure 6). This grass had replaced the previous chaparral of small scrubby oaks, barberries, and acacias, perhaps because the U.S. Forest Service (USFS) had used the seeds of common barley to stabilize vegetation-free soils, which the

Figure 4. The stream after having been ravaged by the floods that occurred after the Willow Fire destroyed most of the hillside and riparian vegetation.

Figure 5. The fiery deaths of the streamside sycamores, oaks, and junipers set the stage for the deep downcutting that took place in the stream bed.

Figure 6. The United States Forest Service planted domesticated barley on the slopes above Deer Creek to slow erosion in the first year after the fire.

Willow Fire had created in abundance. Bill Hart of the Tonto National Forest tells me that it is standard practice to broadcast the seeds of one or another variety of barley in fire-damaged environments on the grounds that barley is a nonpersistent annual. As a result, the introduced grass would be replaced by native plants after a year or so, during which the nonnative barley would keep entire hillsides from sliding down into the creek. My experience tells me that the nonnative barley used in the Mazatzals did indeed quickly disappear. The same thing happened when the Forest Service broadcast barley seed (among other species) in an effort to repair the huge burned area produced by the Rodeo-Chediski Fire in 2002.

Be that as it may, the Forest Service now says that since the mid-2000s, they prefer to use the seeds of native plants as erosion mitigators following wildfires (but European barley, a domesticated nonnative species, was still being used in a low-persistence mix as late as 2012 after a fire in central Arizona). Unfortunately, the seeds of native species are considerably more costly than barley seeds; I hope that, in return for the added expense, the natives do an even better job of soil stabilization than the nonnative exotics. The data on this point are hard to come by, but a number of papers are not encouraging in this regard. In the eastern Cascades of Washington, for example, the use of native seeds did little to reduce erosion or speed the recovery of native plants in the burned area. In fact, in a review of the published accounts on the effects of postfire seeding, a team of researchers led by D. L. Peppin concluded that it did not matter much whether native or nonnative seeds were used; postwildfire seeding did little to reduce erosion, while having a negative effect overall in the reestablishment of the local native flora.

Along the lower stretches of Deer Creek, in places where barley apparently had not been broadcast in the preceding months, a diversity of small native annuals had come back already and were covering what had recently been totally barren, pebble-strewn reaches. The winter-spring rains from 2004 to 2005 had triggered the germination and growth of such delights as bright yellow desert marigolds, magenta owl's clover, and even some barestem larkspurs, an attractive delphinium of modest size whose deep blue flowers contrasted with the largely vegetation-free creek banks. On steep patches of dirt and gravel, albeit in only a few places, clumps of stemless primroses had also taken hold and now sported showers of large white flowers. I suspect, but do not know for sure, that these plants and more were benefiting from the extra nitrogen contained in the soil, courtesy of the dead plants that had been charcoaled and made available for recycling by the Willow Fire. Whatever the reason, their presence helped make the dead trees and gouged stream bed slightly easier to countenance. Although death and destruction were still the dominant features of Deer Creek, the occurrence of plants that were common here before the fire told me that chaparral plants have the ability to rebound after a fiery disaster. A recovery to celebrate for persons with time on their hands.

Returning to Deer Creek

Whether because Sue held to her refusal to revisit the fire-damaged Mazatzals or because I too decided to spend my time walking in the unburned parts of Arizona, it has been well over three years since I last drove up to Deer Creek. My solo walk on this winter's day begins under cloudless blue skies; a light dusting of snow covers the north-running ridge of the Mazatzals. The air is so crisp and cold that I could be forgiven for thinking I was in southern Canada rather than hiking in central Arizona. An assortment of dried brown weeds and grasses covers the flats on the way to the South Fork Trail. Hunters in fluorescent orange vests zigzag across the prickly pear pasture accompanied by their dogs, presumably in pursuit of Gambel's quail.

The hunters went one way and I went another as I headed for the overlook to Deer Creek, which is full of life today, the stream six feet wide in places and in a great hurry to get somewhere. Some of the dead sycamores continue to withstand entropy. They occupy the dry ground littered with rocks left behind by the floods of 2004 and 2005. But the rocky islands are no longer completely bereft of vegetation; instead, patches of dried weeds and grasses have taken their place among the stones and fallen trees.

Here and there in a tiny side channel, a water pocket has frozen, forming a thin, elevated sheet of almost transparent ice decorated in fantastic white geometric shapes. On hillsides where some prickly pear pads have decayed, crystalline hoarfrost covers each wavy thin element of what I assume must be the internal skeleton of the pads. Little tufts of pale brown grass are similarly ornamented with minute ice crystals.

As I approach the vigorous south fork of the creek, I realize that I am going to have to decide whether to remove my boots time and again and tiptoe gingerly across the rocky stream bed or just plunge in the shallow water and say the heck with it, which is what I did after just one icy attempt at a barefoot crossing. My feet became very wet, but I saved considerable time by keeping my boots on during stream crossings.

To my delight, a few sycamores have sent suckers up from the root balls of what was left of the burnt parent trees. These saplings produced leaves that have fallen in a memorial wreath of sorts around the torched trunks, blackened from the ground up during the big fire. The leaves range in color from yellow-green to dark brown; many are edged in white ice that makes them look like botanical jewelry (figure 7).

It is not just sycamores that have come back in the four-plus years since the Willow Fire. The still-lifeless junipers are now surrounded by globe mallows, admittedly not in flower yet, but in the months ahead, these shrubs will bring the color orange back to the Mazatzals. A few willows have colonized the stream edge in places; shrub live oaks abound, some having grown three feet tall since their reestablishment; and some mesquites have taken hold on higher ground. Patches of prickly acacias crowd together around isolated barberry shrubs. The low but spiny vegetation provides refuge for flocks of sparrows: white-crowned and black-throated, a rufous-crowned sparrow here, a few Lincoln's and one vesper sparrow there, swarms of chipping sparrows, gray-headed juncos, and even a smattering of black-chinned sparrows. This last species is outfitted in its more modest winter plumage (which lacks the black patch about the pink bill) but is still a strikingly good-looking sparrow with its blue-gray and red-brown back. Spotted and canyon towhees, the occasional Bewick's wren, and a multitude of ruby-crowned kinglets make the walk a festival of bird life.

Figure 7. The sycamores that had started to come back by 2008 dropped their leaves, which were outlined in frost in the winter of that year.

The ground is still sufficiently bare in places that I find some aboriginal artifacts that I might otherwise have missed, including what I take to be a stone knife with a lightly serrated cutting edge. The tool stands out in the right angles of its design. Were the makers of these artifacts part of a band that roamed up this canyon just a few hundred years ago, or were they members of the first Arizonans that swept through the state some 12,000 years or so before the present? Or were they left behind by some people of an intermediate culture? Did they ever find their hunting grounds burnt but recovering, or were wildfires such a rarity that environmental recovery was not all that frequent in their day?

What is clear is that almost all of the state was utilized at one time or another by aboriginal people, sometimes by quite a large number of these Native Americans. Not all that far from Deer Creek, to the west of the Mazatzal Mountains, lies Perry Mesa, a grassland ecosystem that has been incorporated in the Agua Fria National Monument, a last-minute gift from Bill Clinton to the American people as he was leaving office in 2000. Because of the number of large pueblos that were built on the mesa, the site has attracted a good many vandals and artifact thieves as well as several competent archeologists and their crews (thank goodness for the latter). The professional pot excavators determined that people were living on Perry Mesa for several thousand years but especially in the period between 1275 and 1450. Although almost no one inhabits the area currently, which is home to some cows thanks to the Bureau of Land Management, the site was once swarming with people. Over 600 years ago, just one of the many archeological sites on what is now a national monument had enough inhabitants to fill an eighty-room pueblo; and one other location contains over 200 petroglyphs. People, lots of them, have been in central Arizona for far longer than we usually imagine.

The occasional humble artifacts that I find, look at, and toss back on the ground speak to the long occupation even of places that look unpromising, to say the least, from the perspective of a modern human. I would not be at all surprised to learn that pueblos have been built and abandoned a very short distance from the south fork. It would be a thrill to find even one petroglyph here. But for the moment, I must content myself with the odd stone tool lying on the rocky ground and the sparrows that are able to make a living in a hard land covered in little sharp-leaved oaks and spiny acacias, plants that can cope with the aftermath of a wildfire.

Spring Revival

May 2009

Another year and half or so has vanished from the calendar, but the time has been put to good use in the once-burned areas of the Mazatzals. Along the stream, the perennial oaks and acacias have added considerable biomass in the form of new spiny stems and pointed leaves, with the result that the riparian zone looks positively green and shrubby on this pleasant May morning. Admittedly, the dead and still standing junipers serve as reminders of the now nearly five-year-old Willow Fire, but they are surrounded by vegetative regrowth of all sorts.

In addition to most trees and shrubs, many other native plants have responded to the occasional rains of winter and spring by flowering to a fare-thee-well (there is not a hint of introduced barley anywhere, nor any need for its soil stabilization services). Yellows are represented in the paperflowers (a daisy with a dense coat of bright yellow flowers that grows close to the ground), gorgeous prickly pear flowers, the blossoms of blue paloverdes (which have the dimensions of a low shrub here in contrast to the big trees found along Sonoran Desert washes some thirty or forty miles to the south), and showy yellow columbines along the creek proper, to name a few. Deep magentas and reds appear in the four-o'clocks, which are represented by three species of *Mirabilis* today, among them the appropriately named scarlet four-o'clock; other red-flowered plants include the Arizona penstemon and the littleleaf ratany. The color blue dominates the modest flowers of the miniature woollystar, which has, despite its small size, fought its way up through large patches of dried red bromegrass (an exotic species here), and the Arizona blue eyes, a member of the morning glory family. Several other species of morning glories contribute the noncolor white to the mix along with white prairie clover, a low-lying legume that sports upright stalks topped with fuzzy pipe-cleaner inflorescences constructed from many tiny white flowers.

Although it is difficult for me to choose a favorite from this multihued collection of flowering plants, I will say that I am very fond of the Colorado four-o'clock. The plant has a delightful generic name (*Mirabilis*) that means, according to *Wikipedia*, "amazing, wondrous, remarkable," which applies without doubt to its large, deep pink, tubular flowers (figure 8). Like many other desert and dry country species, the flowers are fully open only early or late in the day, when they are visited by assorted insect admirers, primarily long-tongued hawkmoths that are attracted to the flowers from a distance by their odor but then zero in on the target when close by, helped by the visual properties of the flower. In at least some cases, hawkmoths can measure the amount of nectar they will find in a flower by analyzing the local humidity resulting from evaporated nectar in the air around the bloom, all the better to forage optimally among the flowers available to them.

If a hawkmoth is prepared to extract the nectar from a flower it has found, it does so by inserting its long proboscis deep into the flower's corolla in search of nectar. The pollen-producing stamens and pollen-receiving stigma of a Colorado four-o'clock extend beyond the tubular corolla, presumably the better to come into contact with a hawkmoth's feeding apparatus or body. In this way, the flowers transfer pollen from their stamens to the insect while also picking up pollen already attached to the proboscis or head of the moth as a result of earlier visits elsewhere to this species.

Research on the Colorado four-o'clock has shown that the more nectar per flower, the more visits to a given plant by hawkmoths. You might

Figure 8. The big showy flowers of Colorado four-o'clock signal that the recovery of Deer Creek after the Willow Fire is underway.

think that this result means that Colorado four-o'clocks should invest in more nectar per flower for pollinators than they actually do. But plants with artificially elevated nectar levels in their flowers encourage pollinators to stay put, visiting flower after flower on the nectar-enhanced individuals. The response of hawkmoths to increased nectar rewards leads to less outcrossing and more selfing, as pollen from one flower on plant A gets picked up and deposited on another flower of the same plant. For species that benefit from being outcrossed, this result is not desirable. Better to provide just enough nectar to get a pollinator to come for a quick feed before moving on with some pollen to another flowering individual where male gametes from plant A have a chance to be placed on the pollen-receiving structure of plant B.

The yellow columbine is another hawkmoth-pollinated plant that is available to those hawkmoths that call Deer Creek home. Like the flowers of the Colorado four-o'clock, the columbine's blossoms are not only gorgeous but also worth studying, not that many botanists have focused their attention on this particular species. One person who has studied the yellow columbine is Russell Miller, who looked at this plant in the Chiricahua Mountains of southeastern Arizona. There he documented that hawkmoths were indeed the major pollinators, as one would expect given the structure of the columbine's beautiful flowers (figure 9), which place their rewarding nectar in long spurs that project back away from the open face of the flower. To secure nectar, a hawkmoth must insert its proboscis deep into the spur, which may lead the moth to contact the stamens and stigma as required for pollen pickup and transfer.

Interestingly, the hawkmoth species most commonly observed at the plant in the Chiricahuas had a proboscis that was about two centimeters shorter than the nectar-containing spurs of the flower. This meant that when these hawkmoths came a-visiting in the evening, they left some of the nectar untouched because they simply could not reach it. There were some rarer sphingid moths in the mountains with longer proboscises capable of poking into the end of the spur. Miller speculated that these species might actually be the better pollinators of the columbine. In this, he was following Charles Darwin, who had proposed that long spurs or floral tubes had evolved as a result of interactions between plants and pollinators. According to Darwin, over the course of evolution of some species, individual plants with longer-than-average nectar spurs favored specialist pollinators with relatively long proboscises, leading eventually to moths with an exceptionally long feeding apparatus, the better to extract as much nectar as possible from the spur or tube. In so doing, the hovering moth was "encouraged" to adopt a position that maximized the pollination chances of the plant.

If Darwin was correct in his explanation for the match between proboscis length and floral tube length, then experimental shortening of the nectar-containing spurs of the yellow columbine should lead to less efficient pollination of the plant. In such cases, the "good" pollinators with long proboscises would be able to extract the nectar reward without getting as close to the flower's stamens and stigma as they would when

Figure 9. Another spectacular flowering plant of streamside Arizona, the yellow columbine.

feeding from floral tubes of normal length. The experiment has been done with some orchids (but not columbines) with positive results (i.e., the results that were predicted to occur). Hard-to-reach nectar at the end of a spur is used by the plant to manipulate the flight behavior of effective pollinators in ways advantageous to the plant as well as to the moth.

A special member of the plant community in bloom along the trail today is Palmer's penstemon, a species the flowers of which lack elegant spurs or floral tubes. This species, however, does have extravagant flower-laden, five-foot-tall stalks, which makes it among the tallest of the forty or so species in the genus *Penstemon* found in Arizona. Each stalk supports a modest number of attractive blue-green leaves close to the ground, while the rest of the way to the top is lined with large, pinkish, globular flowers. These handsome flowers are so attractive that the authors of *A Field Guide to the Plants of Arizona* have written that that Palmer's penstemon is "spectacular." I completely agree.

A distinctive feature of the flowers is a hairy, brush-like rod that projects out of the mouth of the flower and over the middle lip petal (figure 10). This structure is known in botanical circles as a staminode, a sterile stamen that evolved via changes in one of the original five pollen-producing stamens in an ancestral species. The flowers of Palmer's penstemon still have four functional stamens that are tipped with packets or sacs filled with pollen. Visiting pollinators, usually large bees in the case of this species, acquire pollen from the fertile stamens that they carry to another flower, where the pollen may be deposited on the end of the style of that other plant. The style is a slender, elongate stalk that grows out of the ovary of the flower; pollen placed on the tip of the style (which has a name, of course, the *stigma*) will trigger the growth of internal tubes that travel downward through the style, carrying "sperm" to the eggs within the ovary. If all goes well, the ovary's eggs will be fertilized and will mature into seeds within a fruit that forms after the flower petals have been discarded.

So Palmer's penstemons, like all other penstemons, have hermaphroditic flowers with male and female parts for the production and dispersal of their own pollen and the receipt and utilization of pollen from other flowers. But why then do they have that single pollenless stamen, the sterile staminode? If this structure has no pollen-producing capacity, why hasn't it disappeared or at least become reduced in size and therefore cheaper to build, as is true for many apparently useless vestigial devices, like the tailbones found at the end of the human backbone? But instead of becoming smaller, the large staminode of Palmer's penstemon now sports a collection of long golden hairs that occupy a fair amount of space in the entryway to the flower.

Two botanists, Lawrence Harder and Jennifer Walker-Larsen, wondered whether the staminode had taken on another useful reproductive

Figure 10. The gorgeous flowers of Palmer's penstemon provide an intriguing puzzle—what is the function of the hairy staminode that sticks out of the mouth of the flowers?

function even though it was not a pollen producer. They removed the staminode from some flowers of Palmer's penstemon, with the result that fewer pollen were deposited on the stigma when bee pollinators came visiting. By watching how bees interacted with the staminode of intact flowers, the botanists documented that when pollinators clambered over or landed on the hairy part of the staminode, the device moved, and that movement in turn forced the style down onto the thorax of the bee pollinators. As the tip of the style came in contact with the bees' thorax, pollen were transferred to the stigma, with the result that the staminode-bearing flowers gained an egg fertilization advantage. The staminode is an adaptation after all!

Many penstemons, like the Arizona penstemon, are not bee pollinated but instead attract hummingbirds. These red-flowered, bird-pollinated penstemons lack a fuzzy tongue staminode that acts as a lever to push the stigma down on a hummingbird's beak or forehead. Removal of the nonfurry staminode of these species does not reduce the pollination efficiency of their tubular red flowers, and so it appears that this flower part is truly vestigial in these cases. But one does wonder why the useless ex-stamen has not disappeared altogether from the flowers of hummingbird-pollinated species. Is the developmental system that underlies the production of fertile stamens dependent upon genes that have as a nonfunctional side effect the building of a full-size staminode? Or does the staminode of bird-pollinated penstemons provide some as yet still undiscovered reproductive benefit for the members of these species? These questions heighten my appreciation for the aesthetic Palmer's penstemons with their furry golden staminodes, which make the penstemon flowers not only beautiful but intellectually intriguing for those of us who enjoy thinking about adaptation when we look at the attributes of living things.

After the Monsoon

September 2009

T he monsoon of 2009 has come and gone and so have Palmer's
penstemons. The flowers faded and formed fruits long ago, leaving behind dried stalks, some of which have already broken off so that
all that remains is the clump of basal leaves. These plants will probably
survive until the next spring, when they may sprout a new supply of
fresh flower stalks for the occasional hiker to admire.

Some plant species, unlike Palmer's penstemons, flower in both the
spring and fall, provided that each season has been preceded by sufficient precipitation to bring out the best in them. One of the species that
blooms over a broad range of dates, if conditions are good, is Hooker's
evening primrose, a robust plant of medium height with multiple stalks
that can support large numbers of big flowers (figure 11). These bright yellow blooms open in the evening and expire within twenty-four hours, as
is characteristic of members of this genus. Here in midday, many flowers
that presumably opened the previous evening still look reasonably fresh,
but others have collapsed into a twisted mass of withered, dark-orange
petals. Like Palmer's penstemon, the primrose exploits the moisture provided by the creek and so is more or less restricted to the stream bed.

Hooker's evening primrose and many other members of the genus
Oenothera are outcrossed species that benefit from the exchange of

Figure 11. Hooker's evening primrose produces lovely, fresh yellow flowers, which quickly turn reddish and collapse after pollination has occurred.

pollen between plants, a task that requires special pollinators that fly in the dim light of dusk, when the flowers have just opened. Not surprisingly, hawkmoths are ideal pollinators for this species as well as for the Colorado four-o'clock. The moths come around in the early evening to hover by the flowers, which they probe with their absurdly long proboscis. In so doing, they may pick up pollen for transfer to another primrose. In at least some parts of its geographic range, big evening-active bees join the hawkmoths at flowering primroses and thereby also contribute to the movement of pollen between plants. When pollination occurs, hawkmoths and/or bees deposit the pollen they have picked up on a four-branched stigma, an unusual and distinctive structural element of this genus. Because the style is taller than the stamens of the flower, the risk of self-pollination is greatly reduced, which benefits the plant, given that outcrossing must occur if the primrose is to produce viable seeds. In addition, pollinated flowers quickly wilt, in which attitude they are not attractive to either hawkmoths or bees; collapsed flowers tell insects that they contain no nectar and so should be avoided, a benefit to the pollinators and also for the plants, inasmuch as any visitors will concentrate on open flowers still capable of being pollinated rather than those that have already served their reproductive purpose.

In the middle of the creek, I come across a strange form of Hooker's evening primrose. This odd plant has produced a thick paddle-shaped stem about two feet high, totally unlike the long thin stems typical of this species—and most other plants for that matter. The aberrant stem supports a collection of leaves on its upper portion and is lined along the very top with a series of attractive yellow flowers, which are in every way normal in appearance. The paddle-stemmed primrose is vaguely similar to the weird crested or cristate saguaro cactus, which has an arm or a trunk with a flattened, fan-shaped tip. Because these cacti are unusual, they attract attention and even thieves, who try to make off with cristate specimens for sale to collectors who put a special value on these unaesthetic but unusual saguaros. I doubt that the cristate primrose before me would command a high price, but I do wonder what developmental quirk is responsible for this freak of nature and whether similar developmental deviations are responsible for cristate cacti.

In addition to the primroses that have colonized the stream bed, willows are now well established along considerable stretches of the lower stream, especially in places where the water is flowing or at least present in the creek channel. True, the water in these trickles and pools is slowed by the thick, yellow-green algal mats that float there. Perhaps these rather ugly, off-chartreuse algae slow evaporation in the places where the algae are the thickest. But the important thing is that there is water in the stream, either moving aboveground or slipping underground in other stretches. This water surely has helped the riparian sycamores recover, which ought to be grateful and would be if they could speak to us about their environment. Here and there some of the rejuvenated sycamores are nearly twenty feet tall, quite an achievement considering that they had to start from ground zero after the Willow Fire a mere five years ago.

Up on the banks above the stream channel, some of the shrub live oaks have reached a size that is compatible with reproduction. The small green acorns produced by these plants, which are really more shrub than tree, are attractive and no doubt appreciated by acorn consumers, such as the black bears that were said to have been reasonably abundant in the Mazatzals—before the Willow Fire.

I have never seen a black bear along any part of Deer Creek, but today I find a green lynx spider clinging to a flowering purple aster. The spider's green body with little black chevrons on its abdomen blends in well with the greenery of the aster, which may be why I rarely see this little predator on my walks. The spider does not elicit the thrill that a black bear would produce, but finding the animal today confirms that a walk along the creek almost always generates novel experiences of one sort or another. When I check Google for images of the green lynx spider, I find that photographers have posted dozens of excellent pictures of this species on the Internet, probably because the spider is widely distributed and unusually colorful. However, a search for scientific papers on the species and its close relatives yields remarkably little. Here is a common, widespread, and good-looking spider that has been largely ignored by the scientific community. Why? Are there simply too few arachnologists to study even the common spiders of this world?

The Lupine Season

March 2010

As the sixth anniversary of the Willow Fire approaches, I come back for yet another look at Deer Creek. A small, thin, white patch of snow high in the Mazatzals is all that remains of winter snow cover. But the snow that has melted has enlivened the stream once more. The southern branch is flowing energetically (relatively speaking), even past the point where the trail first makes contact with the creek. Sue has come along, having been persuaded to put to one side her past declaration that she would never return to this fire-damaged part of Arizona. Although she finds it challenging to maneuver across the creek in places where a crossing is required, Sue and I both agree that the place is well worth visiting thanks to a colorful array of flowering annuals and small perennials. There are red maids, matte-yellow mustards, and a brilliantly reflective yellow blazing star, white desert anemones, two species of stork's bills, one with pink and the other with blue flowers, and several species of lupines with blue and white flowers (figure 12). Some of the species on this list have leaves that are every bit as visually attractive as the flowers, if not more so, a point that applies especially to the lupines and the Texas stork's bill (figure 13).

Although consuming lupines is said to make cattle ill, especially if the cows eat the seed pods, most of the plants in flower today can be

Figure 12. The hairy leaves of a native lupine growing next to a flowering nonnative stork's bill.

Figure 13. The leaves of the Texas stork's bill are every bit as attractive as the flowers of many plants.

eaten by cows (and humans) in whole or part. The young leaves of the common stork's bill, originally a plant of the Mediterranean region, are supposed to be suitable for those of us interested in food novelties. This highly invasive species has taken over California and Arizona, among other places. The plant appears to have made it up from Baja California on its own without assistance from cattle since the plant's pollen has been found in cores taken from sea bottom sediments just off coastal California that can be dated reliably back to the period prior to the first Spanish settlement in this state. To be precise, the initial appearance of common stork's bill pollen comes from a sediment layer dated from 1755 to 1760, whereas the first Spanish mission was erected in 1769. So overgrazing by Mexican cattle was not necessary to prepare the way for common stork's bill, which was perfectly capable of taking advantage of openings in the "natural" environments found north of Mexico.

One of the attributes of stork's bills that might contribute to its capacity to move into new terrain is its explosive dispersal mechanism. As the long, thin fruit matures and dries out, eventually the panels that compose the outer shell of the fruit separate abruptly, sending the seeds within flying up to a half meter from the parent plant. Variations on this theme are common in the plant world with, for example, the long, thin seedpods of Mexican poppies also splitting open violently at some point after reaching maturity, an event that showers the surrounding area with the minute seeds of these plants. But unlike Mexican poppy seeds, which are on their own after hitting the ground, the seeds of stork's bills are attached to awns—long, thin, coiled devices that expand or contract with changes in humidity. The properties of an awn are such that the apparatus helps the seed drill into the ground, where it has a better chance of germinating. Perhaps these adaptations for dispersal and germination of the stork's bill have contributed to its rapid spread throughout the western United States.

Another spring annual with edible leaves is the red maid, although the Internet sites that promote this plant as food warn us not to eat too many of these plants at one sitting because of their high oxalic acid content. This chemical is said to be a major component of kidney stones, which none of us want to have. The corms of the Papago onions (or blue dicks, as they are also called) could be consumed, but the plants are supposedly protected, so I am not tempted to eat these lilies but would rather photograph their lovely pale blue flowers.

We even encounter a few plants of miner's lettuce, whose little white flowers are nothing to get excited about, but their small round leaves evidently make an excellent salad rich in vitamin C. This fact made the plant popular with the gold miners of 1849, who ate the plant in order to avoid scurvy, a debilitating disease that can be cured by consuming foods with reasonable amounts of vitamin C. Hank Shaw, a modern wild food advocate, enthusiastically trumpets the merits of miner's lettuce, noting that the plant was taken to England long ago in order to pep up British salads.

The list of comestible wild plants that occur in Arizona is a long one probably because the original inhabitants of the land, the Amerindians, were often hungry and keen to extract calories and nutrients from whatever was on hand. They were also alert to the medicinal properties of plants that grew around them and collected a vast array of plant parts to treat assorted ailments. The Spaniards and Anglos who invaded the land more recently must have often been hungry or sick too and thus were happy to take foraging and medicinal instruction from the aboriginal inhabitants of the land whenever they could. Although I know that wild food gathering is enjoying a revival these days, especially in the world of haute cuisine, I will leave the stork's bills, the red maids, and the miner's lettuce alone on the grounds that the Safeway and my own garden can supply me with all the vegetable food I need or desire. I know it is not very adventurous of me, but then again I am neither a starving Amerindian nor a scurvy-threatened miner.

Spring on Deer Creek

Early April 2010

M y previous visit to the stream was so botanically rewarding that I have come back again roughly a month later to see what late spring hath wrought in the Mazatzals. Many of the plants that pleased me on my last walk are still here, and still in flower, although the lupines have also begun to produce their little pea-shaped pods, an indicator of spring's progress.

One notable addition to the flowering plant list is the little goldfields, a yellow aster that covers large areas of the occasionally grazed flat plateau to the east of the South Fork Trail. Although the plants are individually small, the collective effect of thousands of goldfields massed together is to paint the pasture yellow. The large groups of goldfields are reminiscent of other large displays of flowering plants, such as the fields of Mexican poppies that occasionally occur in the Sonoran Desert proper. Presumably, an advantage of synchronized flowering comes from the attraction of large numbers of pollinators, which may improve the odds that any one flowering plant will set seed. Alternatively, or in addition, by flowering together in large numbers, the individuals belonging to this population may reduce the odds that they will be harmed by the local herbivores, whose capacity to devour the flowers of a superabundant species will be swamped by the large number of plants that are reproducing in synchrony with one another.

The effects of flower-eating animals are evident in the many flowers of the winding mariposa lilies that have been, or are being, gobbled up by moth caterpillars. In some cases, a plump green caterpillar lies curled in what is left of the basin created by the upraised petals of the lily, the caterpillar having eaten the majority of the petals in question. The uneaten fresh flowers of this species are pleasing to look at thanks to their large, crisp, white to purplish petals with yellow interior splotches coupled with six prominent stamens with conspicuous whitish anthers. An irresistible sight for a photographer—and apparently also for egg-laying female moths, whose offspring appreciate the flowers in their very different way (figure 14a and 14b).

Below the lily-strewn pasture, the stream is in fine fettle with plenty of algae-free water on the move that looks clean enough to drink. But looks can be deceiving, and I am not tempted to test the bacterial or protozoan levels in the stream. The knowledge that *Giardia* is "a genus of anaerobic flagellated protozoan parasites" of the order Diplomonadida (according to *Wikipedia*) that are eager to take up residence in my lower intestine makes me happy to have plenty of chlorine-rich Tempe city water in my backpack.

The canyon tree frogs of Deer Creek are no doubt pleased to have water of any sort in the stream, although they spend a considerable amount of time basking out of the water on rocks and fallen tree limbs near the creek. I doubt that they are susceptible to giardiasis; the parasite that can make us miserable appears to prefer warm-blooded hosts. There is, however, a species of *Giardia* that specializes in the infection of amphibians. I hope that this species is absent from Deer Creek because frogs, toads, and salamanders of all sorts are lately having a very rough time the world over thanks to habitat losses, fungal infections, polluted water supplies, drought, you name it. Canyon tree frogs have apparently tested positive for a particularly ghastly fungus that in some species causes a disease, chytridiomycosis, which is thought to be a major player in the declines and disappearances of so many species of frogs. Some researchers believe that chytrids are largely responsible for a truly

Figure 14. Winding mariposa lilies produce (a) handsome flowers, which (b) attract consumers like this fat moth caterpillar.

gloomy statistic, which is that on the order of 40 percent of all amphibians in North and South America are currently so rare as to be at risk of extinction. Fortunately, canyon tree frogs do not appear to be devastated by chytrids, which is lucky for them—and for amateur herpetologists hiking along Deer Creek.

One reason why this species may be relatively immune to fungal disease could be related to its fondness for basking out in the open in full sunshine. This behavioral trait may make the skin of basking frogs too hot for the fungus, which does not do well at even moderately high temperatures. My guess is that the frogs are so keen to bask not to destroy fungal infections (which are probably a relatively recent and novel problem for most amphibians) but to achieve body temperatures that make digestion of their food occur relatively rapidly and efficiently, given that food-digesting enzymes work best at moderately high body temperatures.

Because the tree frogs do bask openly on rocks, they inadvertently make it harder for evolutionarily novel fungi to invade their bodies, while making it easier for me to spot them. True, the grey or reddish spotted coloration of the frogs matches that of the rocks they like to sit upon, and their immobility helps them blend into their backgrounds (figure 15a and 15b). But after developing a search image for the species, I discovered that they are here, there, and everywhere, even on boulders up to five meters from water. Some of those that I do not detect initially become alarmed enough as I approach to leave their perches and leap energetically to safety, usually by plopping into the water and diving down to the bottom.

The Deer Creek population of the canyon tree frog occurs in the more northerly part of its very large geographic range, which begins in far southern Mexico and runs north to Colorado and Utah. Given that the frog seems ill suited to travel from one drainage to another, a journey that would usually take the little amphibian through highly unpleasant environments (from a frog's perspective), one might expect the different populations to remain geographically separated over long periods. The more time apart, the more opportunity for different mutations to occur in different populations. The result should be the genetic differentiation of the various populations of the frog in different parts of its range.

Figure 15. Canyon tree frogs sometimes (a) rest on rocks in Deer Creek where they are quite well camouflaged. (b) Some of these delightful tree frogs climb rocks far from the water, where they crouch close to their perches.

When this expectation was investigated by geneticists, they found that, yes, the predicted genetic differences were there, along with some added complexity caused by occasional hybridizations between the canyon tree frog and certain other closely related species that live in the same places. These presumably rare hybridization events introduced novel genes into certain populations but not others. Interestingly, one frog species that apparently hybridized with the canyon tree frog does not look very much like its sexual partner, showing that the species in question do not rely on appearances to pair off. Although "good" species are "supposed" to stay apart reproductively, evidently sometimes they do not.

In addition to the discovery that canyon tree frogs occasionally breed with other species, a comparison of the frog's nuclear genes reveals that the southernmost population of canyon tree frogs in Mexico is so different genetically from other groups of this species that this one population should almost certainly be granted its own species' name. This, despite the fact that the tree frogs in this area look very much like those to the north. In other words, looks can be deceiving when it comes to classifying tree frogs. This point has broad application because some populations whose members all look pretty much the same have been shown to be composed of look-alike but genetically distinct sibling or cryptic species.

Findings of this sort have become increasingly common with the development of techniques for comparing the genetic makeup of subgroups of animals that are widely distributed, like the canyon tree frog. For example, a very common bird of the Southwest is the curve-billed thrasher, a "species" that some persons believe should be split into three. This conclusion is based on the fact that the genetic differences between three geographically distinct populations of the thrasher are so substantial that one could defend calling each population a different species. The difficulties, however, in establishing just how great genetic differences must be before we can call different populations separate species as opposed to subspecies have made evolutionary geneticists cautious about decisions of this sort.

On my way back down to the trailhead, I inspect a curve-billed thrasher nest with its two small, blind nestlings. I do not concern myself whether some other thrashers far to the south should or should not share the same species name with these two youngsters, but I am glad that there are biologists willing to tackle this problem. The shortcut that I am following leads me not only to the thrasher nest but also to a patch of ground littered with discarded clothing lying behind a sheltering stand of junipers that escaped the Willow Fire (figure 16). In the desert proper, far to the south, I have not uncommonly seen similar throwaways, grey trousers, brown work shirts, striped polo shirts, ripped backpacks, the whole lot plastered flat against the ground by entropy and the effects of previous rains. As a result of past experience, I know or think I know that these are the property of illegal aliens, far from their homes in Mexico or Guatemala, undocumented immigrants on the trail to what they surely hope will be decent paying jobs in the Unites States. This is as far north as I have run into the discarded clothing of these persons.

Figure 16. Illegal immigrants from south of the border often discard the clothing they were wearing during the first phase of their journey; it is unusual, however, to find these discards as far north as Deer Creek.

The frequency with which one finds trousers and shirts in Arizona that have been left behind by noncitizens is one marker of human population growth. Mexico has a rapidly growing population that has gone from about eighty million individuals in 1990 to one hundred million or so in 2000; now (in 2016) there are well over 128 million Mexicans, even though the birthrate per Mexican woman has fallen from nearly seven in the 1970s to about two currently. In other words, both Mexican and North American women have achieved a birthrate that approaches the replacement rate (in which two parents produce about two children on average). In Mexico, the abundance of young women in the prime years of reproduction means that the birthrate will continue to exceed the death rate for some time. The simple arithmetic of births minus deaths tells us that the Mexican population is not finished growing by a long shot. In the United States, the relatively large numbers of fertile migrants who come to the Unites States to stay, legally or not, contributes to population growth in our nation, despite the ageing of those already here and the increase in the death rate that this statistic presages.

Discussions of the significance of population growth are rare these days even among ecologists, who might be expected to point out that we live in a finite world with finite resources, a fact that casts doubt on the standard economic position that the market will take care of any future problems associated with a large and growing human population. Two persons willing to rebut the Panglossian economists of this world are Charles Hall and John Day, who argue that there are no substitutes for the fossil fuels that have supplied the energy needs of our exploding population. According to these researchers, when we run out of coal, gas, and especially oil, the human species is going to be in for a rude awakening, and probably not all that many decades down the road, given that fossil fuel extraction has almost certainly peaked with the easy-to-exploit fuels already removed and burned. What we have left are the more difficult-to-recover materials that require more energy to remove, reducing the net energy gained from the remaining fossil fuels when they are taken from the ground.

Even without focusing on fossil fuel extraction and the global warming that is associated with their use, a strong case can be made that we humans have already greatly exceeded the "carrying capacity" of the Earth. Biologists with this view argue that if the current human population were to cease growing today, and if every person on the planet were to enjoy the standard of living of the average American, we would need about five additional Earths to provide the resources needed for all of us to live so high on the hog. This conclusion stems from the knowledge that each American on average consumes goods (food, manufactured items, clothing, and more) that come from harvesting the food, water, minerals, and wood from about ten terrestrial hectares of land (over twenty acres of the earth's surface). Because there are only about twelve billion productive hectares of land in our watery planet, whereas seventy billion would be needed for the current seven billion humans, it should be apparent that unequal national standards of living are going to persist and doubtless become even more unequal in the years ahead.

Even if it were possible through technological innovations still to be discovered to support seven or eight billion people at a uniformly high standard of living, the question is, would we be better off with all these human beings? The nineteenth-century British philosopher John Stuart Mill would have responded with a firm "No." Mill wrote,

> There is room in the world, no doubt, and even in old countries, for a great increase of population, supposing the arts of life to go on improving, and capital to increase. But even if innocuous, I see very little reason for desiring it. The density of population necessary to enable mankind to obtain, in the greatest degree, all the advantages both of cooperation and of social intercourse, has, in all the most populous countries, been attained. A population may be too crowded, though all be amply supplied with food and raiment. It is not good for a man to be kept perforce at all times in the presence of his species. A world from which solitude is extirpated is a very poor ideal. Solitude, in the sense of being often alone, is essential to any depth of meditation or of character; and solitude in the presence of natural beauty and grandeur is the cradle of thoughts and aspirations which are not only good for the individual, but which society could ill do without.

Mill's comments appeared in a book, *Principles of Political Economy,* published in the middle of the nineteenth century about when world population had just passed its first billion. Mill was clearly correct in noting that there was room for the human population to expand. Indeed, when I was born, almost a century after Mill's book was published, the Earth had acquired another billion humans. Since the year of my birth (1942), world population has really taken off, *tripling* to more than seven billion as of 2016. Although most citizens of the United States have the idea that the population of our country has not been keeping pace with global rates of increase, actually here, too, I have been around long enough to see a tripling of the national population (from 135 million when I was born to over 320 million by 2016). Perhaps I will live on to see a near quadrupling of both the national and global populations in my lifetime. If I do make it to 2030, I'll be 88, and the total population of the United States is predicted to be over 370 million then, while that of the entire earth is supposed to come in at over 8 billion, according to the U.S. Census Bureau. Note that it took a century for world population to go from one to two billion, but it only took twelve years for the last billion people to join us here on earth (according to *Wikipedia*). The world will receive the next billion in the next thirteen years, if population forecasts are correct.

Some years ago while visiting Mount Rainier National Park, I came across a car in the car park that was festooned with leftwing bumper stickers, one of which read, "Six billion miracles is enough." This bumper sticker is still available, even though the number of miraculous births and subsequent members of our current population has grown by more than a billion. But whether six or seven and a half billion, most biologists become depressed when they think of the environmental and social consequences of such an overabundance of our fellow man and woman. A loss of solitude is the least of our concerns.

Dodder and Hedgehogs

Late April 2010

Now that spring is drawing to a close in central Arizona, I return again to Deer Creek after an interval of just a couple of weeks for another shot of solitude and to continue admiring Palmer's penstemons, the Colorado four-o'clock, a superb little purplish *Clarkia*, the handsome barestem larkspur, and above all the hedgehog cacti, which are in the midst of a period of synchronized flowering. In addition to these ordinary, albeit handsome, plants, there is another species of a somewhat more sinister nature. I speak of dodder, a parasite, that has produced a messy collection of tan vines that have contacted and wrapped themselves around many low-lying plants by the creekside (figure 17). Where the vines twist around the stem of another plant, dodder inserts specialized cells into the victim, which enables the invasive dodder to siphon off water and nutrients from its photosynthetic host. Thus, it does not need nor does it produce the green leaves of a typical nonparasitic plant. Without green leaves or roots, it lives purely off the plants it wraps up in its tangled vines, which may be why dodders sometimes are known as the devil's-guts, hellbine, witch's shoelaces, or strangleweed. The devil's-guts growing here will invest much of the glucose and other biochemicals stolen from the buckwheats they

Figure 17. A mass of dodder vines attached to low-lying plants near Deer Creek.

have parasitized in making hosts of minute white flowers, the reproductive payoff from its parasitic lifestyle.

You may wonder how dodders, of which there are more than one hundred species, manage to find a suitable plant from which to extract life-sustaining water and biochemicals. As it turns out, after germinating, at least one dodder, *Cuscuta pentagona*, has to locate a host growing no more than four inches away if it is to survive. And locate its prey it does by smelling chemicals naturally given off by nearby plants before the parasite selects a particularly suitable host toward which it grows. Upon contact, it wraps a delicate tendril around the chosen plant. The dodder *C. pentagona* has a distinct liking for tomato plants, so much so that if a piece of rubber is painted with chemicals extracted from tomatoes, dodders belonging to this species will reach out hungrily to embrace the inedible rubber tubing. This fondness for tomatoes creates big problems for tomato growers in California, who lose millions of dollars to the parasitic plant each year.

The almost animalian dodders have been studied by some persons who have asked if the plants forage for victims in an adaptive fashion, favoring those that are able to secure greater amounts of useful materials over others that insist on wrapping themselves around plants that are more resistant or less nutritious. (Note that even tomato plants do not take an attack by dodder lying down. Plants that are twenty days old pump up the production of certain substances, like jasmonic acid, that help the host defend itself against its enemy by making it harder for the parasite to insert its "fangs" into the phloem of the plant where water, sugar, amino acids, and the like are available.) One discovery made by researchers interested in the possibility that dodder "behave" in an adaptive manner takes advantage of the fact that individual parasites may exploit two host species simultaneously (as happens frequently when maturing dodders send out multiple tendrils in search of additional victims). Those dodders that tap into two species of hosts can grow larger than those restricted to donor plants of a single species. This result suggests that if an established dodder has the opportunity to tap into the members of a different host species, it should do so rather than attaching itself to an additional host plant of exactly the same species that it had selected previously.

That dodder may indeed be selective in their choice of plants to supply them with water and nutrients is shown in experimental research with a *Cuscuta europea*, a species the searching tendrils of which will accept (i.e., twine around) stems of hawthorn (a host plant) that is in good condition but will reject (i.e., bend away from) plants that are in poor shape. The work that established this point was done by tying the growing tips of the dodder to the stems of plants of the two types and then monitoring the differing responses of the strangleweeds to these two kinds of hosts. Thus, it appears that in this species of dodder, at least, individual parasites can evaluate the quality of potential hosts *before* beginning to siphon off nutrients from these hosts, the better to invest in growing tissue that will strangle victims likely to repay the investment abundantly.

In contrast to dodders, cacti feed themselves. Today almost every cluster of cactus stems has a dozen or so glorious red-magenta blooms on offer, indicating the plant's ability to support its reproductive efforts. Perhaps this is Engelmann's hedgehog, *Echinocereus engelmannii*, or, if not, a close relative of some sort, such as the pink hedgehog cactus, *E. bonkerae*, which is said to be a "poorly defined species [that] is not always easily identifiable in the field." Certainly, identifying the local cactus here is not easy for me. But as far as I am concerned, the name does not really matter; the gorgeous, large, roselike flowers make pinning a name on the plant more or less inconsequential (figure 18).

Because I am here in the last week of April, when the hedgehogs are flowering vigorously, I get to examine the structure of these flowers carefully. In the center of the flower petals (technically known as tepals), I find a thick, bright green style topped by equally green stigmas that are surrounded by dozens of yellowish filamentous stamens. The stigmas look like a collection of very small, green fingers. Here and there, a bee can be seen helping herself to the nectar beneath the forest of stamens in the flower, and in so doing, the insect is showered with pollen thanks to the ability of the stamens to move in response to contact with a pollinator. In other words, the hedgehog is an example of a plant that behaves in ways that increase the odds that an insect will carry pollen from one individual to another.

Somewhat ironically, the cacti are particularly numerous here in the grazed fields to the east of the mountains. Apparently, degraded semidesert pastures provide excellent habitat for *E. engelmannii* or *E. bonkerae*, whatever it is, perhaps because cows have removed plant competitors of the cacti from these areas but have sensibly refrained from eating the spiny cacti. Another desert-dwelling member of the genus *Echinocereus* in Mexico has been shown to respond positively to "anthropogenic disturbance," by which the authors meant the combined effects of people and their livestock in destroying other plants and tearing up the soil.

Figure 18. The beautiful flowers of a hedgehog cactus, *Echinocereus bonkerae.*

Fire disturbance was not included in the mix of factors that altered the environment of the Mexican hedgehog cactus under investigation. As for the local dark pink–flowered hedgehog cactus, the places where it is especially abundant were not burned by the Willow Fire, which would have probably greatly reduced the local population of this species, judging from the damaging effects of wildfire on assorted hedgehog species in New Mexico and elsewhere in Arizona. According to research botanists, fire and the succulent cacti of the Southwest do not go well together.

There are a great many other species of hedgehog cacti, and one of these has been studied with respect to its potential for dealing with habitat alterations brought on by possible climate change. The question studied by these botanists is whether the cactus can shift its distribution northward in the United States rapidly enough to keep up with the shifting areas where temperatures are suitable for the plant's survival. The species in question is projected to have to move between twenty and seventy-five kilometers a decade to keep pace with the increase in temperatures likely in the next decade, a challenge for the cactus to meet given the likely absence of natural corridors along which seed-dispersing animals might travel to suitable patches of habitat where the cactus could find a new home.

The point here is that although some hedgehog cacti can survive, even thrive, when faced with certain kinds of environmental changes, other kinds of disturbances are probably not good news for these plants down the road. The only thing we can be certain of is that in cactus land there will probably be a plethora of disturbances affecting the remaining natural or seminatural areas in the years ahead.

Golden Eagles

Greater Phoenix is now subject to rotisserie conditions, a phase of the year that will last at least until early October in all probability. Almost everyone in and around the city wishes that he or she could escape to the high country, or to Hawaii, or indeed to almost anywhere else. I settle for Deer Creek, which most definitely is cooler than Tempe but not as much as one would like. Still the stream is flowing in places and the water makes all the difference in terms of aesthetics and life in the high(er) country. Admittedly, the stream often seems to be two parts chartreuse filamentous algae to one part water, with dense mats of the stuff occupying the channel where water still flows. In a few places, the stream has stayed unclogged. There, water striders sit on the surface and cast big tic-tac-toe shadows on the bottom of the creek.

Along the edge of the south fork well into the walk, I find a clump of twining snapdragon on a bank of rocks and dirt up from the stream. The reddish-purple flowers are most beautiful, rather like smaller-than-average snapdragon flowers, which makes sense because both the domesticated snapdragon and the wild twining species were once placed in the plant family Scrophulariaceae, not a particularly aesthetic name for a family known for its handsome flowers. (Now, however, the twining snapdragon has been placed in the Plantaginaceae as a result of

DNA sequence studies that have split many plant groups away from the Scrophulariaceae.)

Naturally, the blossoms attract my attention first and foremost, but upon mature reflection, I realize that the leaves are also good looking, dark green, and almost triangular in shape (figure 19). The leaves are free from blemishes because insect herbivores have left them alone, probably because the plant contains a biochemical called antirrinoside, a protective toxin that repels many plant consumers. The toxin appears to be working well here, but elsewhere the larvae of several moths have been observed eating the leaves of twining snapdragons despite their toxic protective chemistry. Not only do these special herbivores munch the leaves with impunity, they recycle a portion of the nasty biochemical, storing it in their bodies for their own protection against other animals that would eat them.

Time and again, herbivores have evolved the ability to turn a plant chemical that deters most herbivores into a chemical repellent that helps these specialist herbivores survive interactions with *their* predators. Indeed, more than 250 insect species are known to sequester one or another plant toxin in their tissues for use against would-be insectivorous predators. My undergraduate advisor, Lincoln Brower, was one of the first biologists to document the nature of this special relationship between insect herbivores and toxic plants. Brower demonstrated that monarch butterfly caterpillars do not manufacture the protective cardiac glycosides in their bodies but instead acquire these substances from their milkweed food. To establish this fact, he fed monarch larvae cabbage, eventually creating a line of butterflies whose caterpillars could grow to maturity on this unnatural but nonpoisonous food. When these cabbage-reared individuals metamorphosed into adults, they were entirely palatable to captive bird predators, which grabbed the butterflies and ate them with gusto.

In contrast, monarch larvae that feed on the leaves of toxic milkweeds are usually rejected by captive blue jays. Why? Because when monarch caterpillars feed on milkweeds, they, like the moth larvae that consume twining snapdragons, sequester and store the toxic biochemical in their own tissues, which makes them highly unpalatable. When the larvae

Figure 19. Twining snapdragon in flower—a plant that is protected against most insect herbivores because of the poisonous chemicals in its leaves.

transition to adulthood, they carry the plant toxins along with them. The consequences of attempting to eat chemically protected adult monarchs were highlighted by Brower who photographed a captive blue jay that had been induced to eat a portion of a frozen, then thawed, monarch that, as a caterpillar, had fed on a toxic milkweed. After swallowing a chunk of poisonous monarch, the blue jay became, shall we say, an unhappy camper, which it revealed by vomiting. The loss of its meal, captured on film, was a protective response for the blue jay that not only removed the glycosides from its digestive system but also learned from the unpleasant experience of vomiting to refuse to have anything to do with monarchs that Brower subsequently placed in the bird's food dish.

Brower argued that in nature, when a caterpillar-hunting or butterfly-hunting predator grabs a toxic monarch by its wing, it gets a good taste of the bitter poison and so usually releases its "victim" promptly before killing and eating it, much to the benefit of the butterfly. So the nasty glycosides have the function of making monarchs taste so bad that they are voluntarily dropped by most predators. But if a really hungry, naïve jay does actually eat all or part of a glycosidic monarch, it will learn after one trial that these nauseating, bitter-tasting creatures should be left alone. The conspicuous coloration of monarch larvae and adults presumably helps make interactions with these prey memorable for hungry, unschooled predators.

On today's walk along the creek, I find two milkweeds, which are not among the species that Brower studied, although they are members of the same genus (*Asclepias*). One of these, Engelmann's milkweed, has relatively few, thin leaves, so that any one plant can hardly provide much of a meal for a decent-sized caterpillar. The other, the antelope horns milkweed, is a somewhat more robust milkweed with larger leaves, which are possibly more appealing to egg-laying female monarchs and their offspring. In the southeastern United States, the antelope horns milkweed contains very high levels of a toxic cardenolide, and monarch larvae that feast upon the leaves of this species become very poisonous as a result.

Recently monarch aficionados have become sadly aware of the importance of milkweeds for this butterfly because milkweeds (and monarchs) are disappearing from fields in the United States. In the past, one species of milkweed, *Asclepias syriaca*, often grew abundantly in or around agricultural fields, but now the plant is much less common due to the spraying of herbicide on crop plants that have been genetically modified to survive the effects of the herbicide. Milkweeds have not been genetically modified and so are vulnerable to Roundup. Brower believes that the decline in the monarch's food plant is a major reason why the butterfly itself has become far less common than it once was. In 2013, the number of eastern monarchs was believed to have fallen to one twentieth the historical average.

Not only do those milkweeds that are still with us often possess bad-tasting (or worse) biochemicals, they also invest in a network of veins that they fill with a white, milky sap. A small caterpillar that starts to cut into a milkweed leaf with its jaws releases the sticky sap from some leaf veins where the sap had been stored under pressure. So the milkweeds have a double-barreled defense, toxic chemicals that taste terrible to most consumers and sticky latex that gums up the jaws of those larvae that can handle the toxins.

But just as some insects have evolved chemical resistance to the toxic biochemical in certain food plants, so too some have countered the sticky-sap tactic. At least in east coast milkweeds, monarch caterpillars that have grown into the midsized range crawl over to the midvein of a leaf, which they cut with their mandibles, causing the leaf to droop and the latex to come rushing out at the wound. The caterpillar then returns to the outer portion of the leaf where the herbivore can feed freely because the latex network in the outer part has been inactivated thanks to the strategic midvein cut. There is a war going on out there between plants and plant consumers.

All along Deer Creek plants of another family, the Euphorbiaceae, are also flourishing. These species, like the milkweeds, employ a sticky, milky sap as a defensive chemical. Most of the euphorbs, however, are small, ground-hugging plants, some barely an inch or two high, with great quantities of minute white flowers. Even without the gluey fluid they release when a skinny stem is plucked, their small size would seem to make them an uneconomical mouthful for most local herbivores. If there are some very small insects capable of converting a euphorb into offspring, they don't seem to do much damage to any of the several members of the family found along Deer Creek. But it probably does not hurt to have a supply of sap on hand with which to deter or incapacitate creatures that would eat the plant.

As I march back next to the creek, I take my eye off the streamside flora long enough to spot a pair of golden eagles, a great rarity here. The two birds fly high overhead initially, but one drops down to perch in a fire-killed juniper on the north-facing slope to my right. The eagle holds a snake in one foot and plucks at the flesh of the reptile in a halfhearted manner before launching itself into the air to follow its partner on a journey south.

Great Spreadwings

October 2010

More than six years have now passed since the Willow Fire. The morning is warm at the trailhead, in fact surprisingly warm for the end of October. But the air is clean and the sky is blue. Walking toward the stream, I hear gunshots in the distance. Then I see some quail hunters and a dog on my far left in among the scrubby acacias. I continue forward. But when I reach the stream, a new volley of gunshots comes from a point very close by. What I would not give for a bit of solitude or at least freedom from gunfire today. I call out, pleading with the hunters to hold their fire. One man appears on the crest of the hillside and waves—which I take to be an indication that he has heard my request and will honor it. I move ahead quickly full of hope. Suddenly more gunshots explode just off to my left. I yell out again, agitating for a temporary cease-fire. I hear an affirmative grunt, or think I do, and so hurry upstream as fast as I can go to remove myself from the range of accidental bird shot.

The creek is dry in its lower part, but eventually I encounter water aboveground here and there. A sharp-shinned hawk dashes away in hurried flight, while a couple of canyon towhees squeal as they dive from the cover of one cluster of chaparral oaks to another.

A plant species that I cannot recall seeing in abundance before is the longleaf false goldeneye; the yellow daisy-like flowers of the plant brighten large swaths of the north-facing hillside near the creek. False goldeneye is apparently toxic to cattle, which is fine by me and may help explain its abundance on the hillside across the way. In addition to the false goldeneye, I encounter large numbers of purple-flowered tansy-asters belonging to the genus *Machaeranthera* as well as a goldenrod, also members of the daisy family (Asteraceae), a highly diverse group with more than 20,000 species worldwide. Only the orchid family may have produced more species than the daisies, but their representatives are absent along Deer Creek, whereas daisies are abundant.

Among the other common flowering plants today are some morning glories, including the red star with its small, intensely red flowers growing on the edge of the creek (see figure 38). Although all morning glories are listed as noxious weeds in Arizona, whether they are native or non-native, it is very difficult for me to believe that this morning glory with its beautiful flowers of very modest dimensions is truly a bad guy. The fact that the seeds of at least some morning glories are highly toxic to cattle probably explains why the authorities in Arizona have lumped all morning glories together before tossing them into the unwelcome bin. Inasmuch as I am neither a cow nor a cattle rancher, however, I am free to admire the red star and several other related species that grow along Deer Creek, each belonging to the large and diverse morning-glory family, the Convolvulaceae. Interestingly, dodders also belong to this family, a conclusion reached by geneticists who compared certain regions of DNA in morning glories and dodders, a comparison that revealed key genetic similarities between these superficially very different plants. At one time, the dodders were placed in a family of their own but no longer, thanks to the work of botanical geneticists who have examined the DNA sequences of morning glories and their potential relatives.

Although the stream is not flowing in its lower reaches, higher up water slips quietly downhill, making the long filaments of green algae in the creek wave ever so slightly. I find the first canyon tree frogs of the day about an hour's walk from the trailhead. One of the little grey amphibians is perched high on a fallen limb near the stream, a position that must have required the frog to do a considerable amount of gymnastic climbing. It sits in the full sun and is reluctant to move when I come closer.

I eat my lunch at the stream, an apple, a muesli bar. Across from my seat, a fairly large black-necked garter snake slithers and slides through a rock pile bordering the creek. One rubyspot damselfly perches on rock while near the little riparian willows, small numbers of *Archilestes grandis*, a big damselfly as implied by its scientific name, perch or flutter slowly from one rock to another.

One fifteen-foot-tall willow tree that leans out over the water has attracted a crowd of great spreadwings, as this damselfly is sometimes known to English speakers. All the damselflies here are paired, the male in front holding the female by her "neck" with his abdominal claspers (figure 20). Many of the females grasped in this manner have inserted the tip of their abdomens into the thin trunk or limbs of the willow on which they have assembled. They are forcing their eggs into slits in the wood. When the eggs hatch, the tiny immature damselflies will tumble into the water below and, with luck, begin the long process of growth and maturation that will eventually result in their metamorphosis from an aquatic nymph to an airborne adult.

The damselflies have crowded together, the females hard at work laying eggs, the males stoically holding onto their partners, which prevents these paired females from being "captured" by single males that would insist that these females copulate again. I verify that single females will attract unmated males by watching an unpaired male fly to and attempt to grasp a dead female that has been killed by a jumping spider in the willow. The spider, a member of the species *Phiddipus johnsoni*, is feeding on the female, which dangles from the mouthparts of the predator, but for the male spreadwing, the dead female is still alluring. He twists and turns trying to make appropriate contact with the moribund damselfly before giving up and flying off.

An unpaired female would almost certainly make herself available to a searching male, leading to a copulation, which damselflies and dragonflies achieve in a manner unique to this order of insects, the Odonata.

Figure 20. A pair of giant spreadwings next to a large female praying mantis; the male damselfly uses the claspers on the tip of his abdomen to grasp the female damselfly, which is inserting her eggs into the stem of a willow that is growing next to the water.

After a receptive female has been grabbed by her "neck," she twists the tip of her abdomen around to reach the male's "penis," which is located on the underside of his abdomen far from the sperm-producing apparatus at the tip of his abdomen. The male will have earlier placed his sperm on this little pedestal; in the wheel-position, the female guides the tip of her abdomen over the "penis," in which position her partner's sperm become available to her.

But before this happens, some male damselflies and dragonflies use their structurally complex penis to reach into the internal sperm storage organ (the spermatheca) of a mate. There, the penis—or *aedeagus*, as it is labeled by pedantic entomologists—hooks any sperm within the spermatheca. As the male withdraws his aedeagus, the other male's sperm are removed from the female. Only then are the current partner's own sperm released to flow into the spermatheca of the female, where they may eventually be used to fertilize the eggs she lays while the male continues to hold the female in the manner of the great spreadwing or hover near her, as do some other damselflies and dragonflies, in order to "protect" her from the attentions of rival males.

The large numbers of great spreadwing pairs in the willow completed their copulations some time ago, and the males guarding their mates may be in the process of being rewarded if their mates are using their sperm to fertilize the eggs they are laying. (Female insects can control the release of stored sperm so that their eggs are fertilized as these pass down the sperm-containing oviduct prior to being laid.) But why are so many spreadwings assembled in this one willow? Perhaps it is ideally suited for the eventual cascade of newly hatched damselflies into the water of the stream. Or alternatively, the damselflies have clustered together to reduce the chances that they will be eaten by predators eager to take advantage of their vulnerability when ovipositing in tandem. The fact that one jumping spider has taken a female and another spider is roaming about within the willow supports the notion that damselfly pairs are at risk of lethal attack. Moreover, I then see a very large brown praying mantis standing only a few inches from a tandem pair. The fact that the mantis just stands there ignoring the nearby damselflies suggests to me that it is no longer hungry, probably because it has already eaten a sufficient number of damselflies to satisfy its appetite. If so, the recent deaths of the prey species now make it relatively safe for the remaining pairs of spreadwings to oviposit in peace.

The "dilution effect" is one of the commonest tactics employed by animals against their predators. If prey aggregate in large groups, and predators are scarce, then safety in numbers results. The more prey present, the lower the odds that any one individual will be among the unlucky ones killed by the predator or predators able to find the assembly of edible victims.

After photographing the great spreadwings until I am satiated, I begin the return trip downstream. Here and there, I spot single damselflies perched on rocks, not great spreadwings but other considerably smaller species in more subdued greys and purples. On my way, I am also entertained by several grasshoppers in the riparian zone. Some species are nicely camouflaged, like the green bird grasshopper that sits without moving among the equally green leaves of shrub live oaks. But some are far more conspicuous, like a jet-black medium-sized grasshopper that I find basking in the open on a large rock. When I flush the hopper, it jumps into flight that suddenly exposes its bright red underwings, which are concealed when the hopper is at rest. Appropriately enough, this species goes by the common name the red-winged grasshopper. After flying a short distance, the red-winged hopper I am watching abruptly folds its wings and drops like a stone into low vegetation covering the ground. So in a matter of a few seconds, this individual has gone from being visually obvious but black, to visually obvious thanks to its striking red wings, and then back to black again before slipping out of sight among some concealing plants. If I were a grasshopper hunter, I might well find all these changes in appearance and behavior more than a little confusing, just as bird predators may become baffled by the changes in the appearance of underwing moths.

The red-winged grasshopper is not the only grasshopper along the creek that employs something like the underwing strategy. Another hopper has a common name, Wheeler's blue-winged grasshopper, that tells of its hidden blue underwings (figure 21). This species is not nearly as conspicuous as the red-winged grasshopper, and indeed, it appears to prefer to hide rather than to confuse if it can get away with sitting still. On a reddish or brown background, the insect is nicely concealed all the more so because of the thin, tan lines on the edges of its upper wings plus a bright white rectangle lower on its wings. Permit me to speculate that both elements help break up the grasshopper's outline, with the tan lines resembling pale weed stems (inedible to grasshopper predators needless to say), while the white patches draw attention away

Figure 21. Wheeler's blue-winged grasshopper, *Leprus wheeleri,*
utilizes two tricks to combat its predators: the first is the white spot
on its forewings, which draw attention away from the rest of the body
and the head of the insect; and the second involves the blue underwings of the grasshopper, which are exposed only when the animal
takes flight but then are hidden again when the insect lands.

from the head of the animal. Should, however, a predator fail to be dis-
tracted by the insect's wing pattern, Wheeler's blue-winged grasshopper
can fly up, exposing its blue hind wings briefly before dropping out of
the air, hiding its blue underwings again, and resuming the largely cryptic behavior of holding still unless closely approached.

The afternoon is well advanced by the time I near the trailhead. There
I meet a fellow hiker heading the other way with a classy walking stick
in each hand. He tells me that he regrets his late start up the trail. I sym-
pathize with him after a fashion, but to be honest, I am content to have
had the trail, the local insects, and the riparian plants almost entirely to
myself today.

The Puzzle of Dioecy

January 2011

In the early morning on this winter's day, the pasture that leads to the south fork of the stream is completely in the shade, a somber grey with a smattering of isolated green junipers, the few that were left after the Willow Fire, dotted across a low, dark ridge to the northwest. Far back from the shaded pastures, the mountains to the north look pink in the morning sunshine that illuminates and washes out every gully and ravine.

It's cold this morning, and a tiny patch of crusty snow lingers in the space between two rocks near the trail. The leafless willows in the sunlight look white and icy with their multitude of upright limbs and stems. The stream is flowing far down the canyon this morning, the water clear and clean, no algae in sight. By the water's edge, a messy pile of white bird feathers litters the ground, the last resting place of a dove or jay surprised while drinking, perhaps by a Cooper's hawk that plucked its victim at the spot. Just upstream, the water spills over a little rock ledge and vigorously splashes into a pool formed by the modest waterfall.

The plants of Deer Creek are restrained today. The sycamores and willows are leafless; the smaller perennials and annuals are in hiding. I do find one patch of blue dicks that have sent up their thin green leaves as a prelude to producing their flower stalks. Also, a few mosses have formed thin archipelagos of bright green in crevices on the rock walls by the creek. Some grasses lie matted but green nonetheless among the stones by the water. But that's about it except for a willow that has managed to generate one line of pale grey buds along a stem.

A major exception to the January rule of botanical dormancy is the silk tassel bush, a small tree or large bush that has been placed in the genus *Garrya*. The shrub is flowering profusely today, having grown clumps of pale tassels that dangle from the tips of its branches in an appealing manner (figure 22). The tassels that catch my attention have small yellow protruding stamens, each set part of the line of flowers that compose an elongate male inflorescence. The female plants have smaller, less aesthetic reproductive parts. In other words, the silk tassel bush is a dioecious plant, in which male and female flowers are found only on separate plants. Only 6 percent of plant species are dioecious, whereas the vast majority are hermaphroditic, with flowers that combine both male and female components (the pollen-producing stamens and the pollen-accepting stigma).

The existence of such different kinds of sexually reproducing plants raises many evolutionary questions. The relative rarity of dioecy suggests that this kind of system evolved from the far more common hermaphroditic mode, but if so, why? Several competing ideas have been proposed ever since Charles Darwin tackled the problem. Darwin was convinced that plants had evolved any number of adaptations that promoted outcrossing, with dioecy being yet another such device. When an entire plant produces either male or female flowers, there can be no risk of any one plant's flowers becoming self-pollinated. Plants that devote themselves to female flowers can only generate offspring in the event that the flowers receive pollen from entirely different individuals. In contrast, hermaphroditic flowers could (and sometimes do) pollinate themselves with pollen that they themselves have produced.

The outcrossing hypothesis has been tested by predicting that insect-pollinated dioecious plants will attract small generalist pollinators prone to remaining on a single plant gathering nectar (*or* inadvertently pollen) for some time. These pollinators would boost the chances of selfing by plants with hermaphroditic flowers, but not if they were

Figure 22. A tassel composed of male flowers of the silk tassel bush, a species in which some plants have only male flowers while others produce only female flowers.

foraging at a dioecious plant with only male or female flowers. Should an insect carrying pollen from a male plant then visit a plant that had made only female flowers, outcrossing could result. Some researchers have found that generalist pollinators visiting dioecious plants do not discriminate between plants with abundant male flowers versus those with smaller, less productive female flowers, a response that makes outcrossing more likely in these cases. This finding makes the Darwinian outcrossing hypothesis more attractive.

However, the silk tassel bush is apparently wind pollinated, making explanations of its dioecy based on the behavior of insect pollinators completely irrelevant. If the ancestors of this species were especially prone to inbreeding for whatever reason, then the evolution of separate sexes might have been adaptive no matter how pollination was effected in these plants. In fact, for wind-pollinated plants, there is no special advantage in having both male and female elements in the same flower, whereas plants with insect-pollinated flowers can often gain by having both components, so that as pollen are picked up from the flower's stamens, other pollen from different flowers can be transferred to that flower's stigma by insect visitors.

For wind-pollinated plants in particular, the evolution of separate sexes within a species could have any of several advantages other than increasing the likelihood of outcrossing. For example, if pollen were less expensive to produce than, say, seeds or fruits, then environmentally stressed plants with male flowers might still be able to make large numbers of "cheap" pollen and, in so doing, pollinate female flowers on other plants. If the female plants grew in lower-stress habitats, they could afford to invest in the large seeds or fruits that cost them more to produce and maintain than pollen, a hypothesis that has been suggested for the dioecious jojoba of the nearby Sonoran Desert.

Or if a plant's reproductive success were essentially a function of the number of pollen produced, then individuals that directed their resources strictly to the making of pollen rather than shunting a portion of these resources to ovule production could do better when competing with individuals whose flowers (some or all) were hermaphroditic. In dioecious plants, pollen-producing (male) plants are in fact "trying" to outdo others of their sex in securing opportunities to fertilize the egg cells of other (female) plants.

There are other ideas about the adaptive value of dioecy, but the main point here is that this relatively rare mating system in plants really deserves an explanation or explanations, which have been a challenge to produce and test. Less baffling is the observation that silk tassel bushes produce bad-smelling leaves that are distasteful to human consumers but still recommended by herbalists for certain medical conditions. Indeed, one such healer, Paulina Nelega, speaks on the Internet of the curative effects of tinctures of silk tassel bush leaves and stems but advises that the concoction only be taken briefly and then only if a consumer is experiencing acute pain, such as the sort associated with menstrual cramps. Given the apparent bitterness of the tea, most persons probably need little encouragement to stop drinking the stuff in the absence of some compelling medical reason.

The bad smell and taste of this shrub surely have not evolved to deter consumption by herbalists and their clients but rather to repel herbivores, like rabbits and deer, in the habitats where the plants occur. The plant is said to be avoided by leaf-eating creatures almost certainly because its leaves are loaded with chemical repellents and/or toxins of one sort or another. I found one author who spoke of the diterpenoids of the silk tassel bush; the very name diterpenoid sounds ominously toxic. So here we have yet another plant that fights destructive would-be consumers with unpleasant compounds of various sorts. "Better things for better living through chemistry" seems to be the motto for most of the plants growing along Deer Creek. "Better things for better living through dioecy" is the motto of only a handful of these plants.

Deer Brush and Recovery After Fire

April 2011

What a difference between the day when I was last here, when the area appeared pale in the cold, hard light of winter, and today, when the creek and the surrounding hills are positively aglow with the warm light of an April day. The leafless, white-barked saplings shivering along the winter stream have become green-leaved willows and exuberant sycamores that seem to be growing taller by the minute. Many plants are in flower, especially the yellow columbines by the edge of the water, which splashes downhill in a seemingly cheerful mood.

Deer brush has also responded to the warmer temperatures by producing large numbers of spikes of attractive white flowers (figure 23). The name of this plant, which is indeed eaten by mule deer, seems highly appropriate for a place called Deer Creek. The widespread distribution of deer in Arizona is no doubt one reason why "my" Deer Creek is only one of several places in the state with *deer* in the name, including at least three other Deer Creeks as well as one Deer Spring and one Deer Lake (at a minimum). There is even a Deer Creek Village, a modest development south of Payson, well to the north of the South Fork Trail.

Admittedly, I have only rarely seen deer along this trail, although they must be hiding out somewhere in the mountains, perhaps coming down in the evening to drink and forage in the relatively lush riparian

Figure 23. The leaves of deer brush are not only edible to mule deer but this nitrogen-fixing plant also may help restore the soil of burned areas.

zone, which continues to recover after nearly seven years of freedom from fire. The deer brush here are large, almost luxuriant, shrubs with untouched leaves and stems, suggesting that deer are not feeding on the plant, at least not in the lower reaches of the stream. Despite the probable presence of certain alkaloids, which occur in at least some members of this large genus of plants, certain species of *Ceanothus* are reasonably edible and as such they are in fact highly popular with cattle in places where cows are free to graze on native shrubs. This genus of plants also attracts small songbirds that like to hide their nests within the dense assemblage of stems and leaves offered by mature deer brush.

Deer brush is also one of the many plant species that form an alliance with microorganisms to the benefit of both parties. In the case of *Ceanothus*, the plant's roots provide "habitat" for nitrogen-fixing bacteria that turn inert atmospheric nitrogen gas (N_2) into ammonia (NH_3) that the plant can use to meet its metabolic needs for nitrogen. This key element is, for example, essential for the production of amino acids, which comprise the building blocks of proteins, which play so many critical roles in the metabolism of all living things. Without the nitrogen-fixing bacteria in its roots, deer brush would presumably be handicapped in a host of ways.

Because deer brush has access to ammonia and the nitrogen derived from this compound, the plant can provide usable nitrogen to other plants around it when this material leaks out of its roots or when its roots and stems decay. This ecological effect takes on special significance after a wildfire because although organic nitrogen is present in the ash that falls upon the ground when plants are burned, much of this valuable substance is lost when nitrogenous compounds are volatilized during intense fires. Furthermore, after the wildfire, erosion may carry the ash with its nitrogen load downslope to a stream to be removed by flowing water, depleting the nitrogen available to growing plants on hillsides. As a result, nitrogen fixers, like deer brush, could be important players in a postfire world as they begin to grow again and their bacterial symbionts begin to supply other plants with growth-promoting nitrogen. Whether or not the local deer brush shrubs have contributed to the revival of the Deer Creek ecosystem, it is clear that the region is well on the road to recovery, a pleasure to see and a testament to the ability of the chaparral here to spring back from the devastation it experienced during the Willow Fire.

Mites, Glochids, and Thunderstorms

July 2011

When I set out, it is a hot, sunny summer morning. In the foothills of the Mazatzals, the local prickly pear cacti have produced an attractive crop of large red fruits (figure 24). In the past, I have sampled a prickly pear fruit or two by first carefully skinning the fruit in order to avoid the spines, large and small, on the skin. The interior flesh is, I can report, sweet and entirely edible, although the seeds, which are large and numerous, are not.

It seems odd that the cactus would manufacture such large sugar-rich fruits and yet protect them from consumers with things like glochids, the very small barbed spines on the fruits that detach themselves easily to impale the lips of cactus consumers. After all, the point of making edible fruits is to ensure that they are eaten, ideally by an animal that will carry the seeds away within its gut to be later deposited some distance from the parent plant, often in a nourishing pile of dung. In other words, edible fruits are typically bribes for seed dispersers. The presence of painfully discouraging spines on large, edible, bright red fruits is then something of a paradox.

Daniel Janzen has made the case that we cannot solve this puzzle without an awareness of the evolutionary effects of the big herbivorous mammals that once roamed the Americas a mere 12,000 years ago but

Figure 24. The small spines (glochids) of prickly pear fruit may have helped ensure that these large, attractive fruits were eaten only by large animals capable of dispersing the seeds of the fruit some distance from the parental plant.

which are now sadly extinct. Janzen argues that the fruits of cacti are almost certainly in large measure the evolved product of grazing by the mastodons and mammoths, the giant ground sloths, and the armadillo-like glyptodonts that once lived in places where cacti still grow. These creatures would have been ideal seed dispersers with tough mouths able to harvest and swallow entire fruits in large numbers before moving off to deposit their feces in quantities that would have contained vast numbers of undigested seeds. Many of the remaining prickly pear fruit eaters, such as jackrabbits, not only consume far fewer fruits per day than a mastodon would but they also often crush and kill the seeds in the fruits they select rather than processing them rapidly through their digestive system before defecating them as intact plant propagules.

Moreover, although mammals are generally color-blind, raising questions about the adaptive value of red-colored fruits, Janzen speculates that the megafauna may have been able to discriminate between red (ripe) and green (unripe) cactus fruits. This ability would have enabled them to select the most calorie- and nutrient-rich fruits rather than consuming unripe fruits, a trait that has benefitted the cactus too—if its goal were to promote the dispersal of its mature seeds. Although the glochids on cactus fruits might deter or slow down smaller consumers, Janzen believes that they would not have stopped huge ground sloths and the like, particularly if these herbivores found ripe cactus fruits a highly desirable resource. (In South Africa, elephants find the mature fruits of some [introduced] spiny cacti irresistible.)

Whatever the evolutionary reason, the fruits of the Deer Creek prickly pears are much larger and far more appealing (once the glochids have been removed) than, say, the fruit of the sugar sumacs growing near the creek. These attractive plants with large evergreen leaves have clusters of small, slightly acidic fruits that can be used in "lemonades." I wonder what creatures are attracted to these fruits, which are conspicuously red. Are the local thrashers and towhees taken by the offerings of sumacs? Do they pass some of the sumac seeds through their digestive systems without destroying the seeds? Do some of the dispersed seeds then have a chance to germinate and produce a seedling sumac?

The sugar sumac does not seem to have attracted the attention of botanists and ecologists to the same extent as prickly pear cacti, but two persons working with the U.S. Forest Service did establish long ago that an intense wildfire appears necessary if the seeds of *Rhus ovata* are to germinate in the soil, at least in the chaparral of California where wildfires are of regular occurrence. Perhaps the Willow Fire enabled the quiescent seeds of the sumac to germinate here in central Arizona.

Some of the plants near the creek are still in flower rather than having reached the fruiting stage. One of these is the sotol or desert spoon, a relative of the agaves, but a distinctive member of the group whose leaves are thin and many. In Mexico, the central core of the plant is sometimes harvested, cooked, and processed to make a mescal-like alcoholic beverage. Here in Arizona, the plants are left to their own devices.

A mature (possibly fifteen-year-old) sotol on a bluff overlooking the low canyon carved by the creek has sent up a ten-foot stalk, the top four feet of which are densely packed with yellow-green flowers. The long wait before reproducing by generating a flower-bearing stalk is one of several traits that has been used to demonstrate that sotols are related to agaves, which do much the same sort of thing. And just as the flowers of agaves are extremely attractive to a variety of pollinators, so too the sotol's flowers have succeeded in drawing in hundreds, if not thousands, of honey bees, as well as a smattering of big black carpenter bees, all eager to harvest the rewards available in those flowers. Judging from the abundance of foraging bees with full pollen baskets on their hind legs, this sotol is a plant with male flowers (pollen producing only). In other words, the sotol offers another example of a dioecious species in which the two sexes are segregated, each sex associated with a different kind of plant. Thus, the honey bees will have to find a female plant elsewhere if they are to act as pollinators, but given the numbers on the flower stalk, some will surely come across a plant of the other sex. The bees' enthusiasm for the male plant might stem from the quantity of pollen they can harvest from this single inflorescence or, alternatively, from the scarcity of floral resources available to them from the relatively few other species of plants that are in flower in the middle of the summer.

In the course of my walk, I notice that clouds have replaced the blue skies that had been overhead. From these clouds comes a rumble of thunder, which prods me to pick up my pace. I am not prepared for rain. Even more emphatically, I am not prepared to serve as a lightning rod.

As I scurry along, I nonetheless pause when I encounter a velvet mite, a very big mite as mites go, which is to say perhaps a little larger than a quarter of an inch long. Some members of the genus reach a maximum size of nearly one-half inch, which qualifies them as the largest mites in the world. The mite that caught my eye is almost certainly *Dinothrombium magnificum*, an entirely appropriate name for what is an admittedly small but thoroughly magnificent creature, the body of which resembles a slightly rumpled piece of fluffy red velvet (figure 25). Any animal so conspicuously red must be unpalatable, and from what I have read, I gather that they do indeed taste bad, certainly to one foolhardy human reporter (not me) who tried to consume a specimen.

Just as impressive as its size and color is the news that the mites only come out very, very briefly each year during the summer rainy season to

Figure 25. A red velvet mite that is moving about on the surface following a thunderstorm in the area. This species comes aboveground only for a very short period each year.

hunt for winged termites, which use a shower in the desert as a signal to leave their natal burrow and fly away before landing some distance from their old home. They then toss off their wings, mate with a termite of the opposite sex, and then start a burrow in the ground with their partner in attendance. But if a mite finds and grasps the would-be king or queen, it is curtains for the termite, the body contents of which provide calories and nutrients for the mite to fuel its search for a mate of its own. The mite has only an extremely limited time in which to accomplish these critical tasks, given the very few days on which winged termites come aboveground for their quick bout of sexual activity. In fact, Lloyd Tevis and Irwin Newell found that many individuals of a related species left their shallow burrows for just a few hours on *one* day after a rain and then returned to spend a year (or more!) underground before emerging again for another microbout of termite hunting.

Figure 26. An isolated thunderstorm dumping water on the chaparral not far from Deer Creek.

Tevis and Newell's study of *Dinothrombium pandorae* in California was published in 1962 in *Ecology*, a very well-known journal in biological circles, but since that time it has been cited only eleven times, without ever stimulating a similar study of the natural history of another member of the genus. I find this remarkable given the abundance and worldwide distribution of species of *Dinothrombium* mites. You might think, or at least I might think, that a conspicuous creature of this sort with a strange and wonderful life history would attract the attention of one or two ecologists or acarologists, but no; velvet mites remain largely unstudied and unappreciated as they wait quietly in their burrows for the special combination of climatic events that triggers their exceptionally short annual walkabouts.

Down the trail I go, not thinking of mites and the shortcomings of acarologists, but rather hoping to reach the trailhead as quickly as possible without being fricasseed. I seem to be walking right into a monsoon shower on my left, judging from the volume of the thunder coming from the dark clouds there. But either the storm veers off or the trail turns away from the danger, much to my relief, which is only temporary once I realize that a much larger storm cell now occupies the zone just to my right. The white sheets of rain that I see there tell me that I am probably going to get wet. The cracks of lightning and accompanying thunder tell me that the experience of walking through the storm is not going to be pleasant (figure 26).

I hurry forward nonetheless, hoping to be lucky. And my wishes are met. The storm drifts off, safely pushing the showers away from me, making the lightning and thunder less ominous, keeping me dry and in one piece. I am appropriately grateful for having avoided electrocution while on the way to my car.

A Day Full of Predators

September 2011

On this sunny day after the end of the monsoon, *Dinothrombium* mites are not out hunting unlucky termites. But other predatory invertebrates make an appearance and, in so doing, enliven the hike up and down South Fork Trail. Some of these are as unmistakable as the tarantula that is hiking across the trail on its eight long and hairy legs. This is the season when male tarantulas march off in search of females to inseminate, which is presumably what this mildly intimidating but essentially harmless spider intends to achieve by moving about during the day. The tarantula that has made my day more memorable is probably *Aphonopelma chalcodes*, one of the more common of the several dozen species of tarantulas found in Arizona (figure 27). However, despite its relative abundance, *A. chalcodes*, like red velvet mites, is not a popular research animal, perhaps because like the mites, it remains underground for the vast majority of the year and is largely nocturnal when it is active, a time when most biologists tend to be in places other than the desert.

Male tarantulas typically require a decade or so to reach maturity, which is when they also reach the end of their lives. Should a male encounter a potentially receptive female before his demise, she may greet him by trying to, and apparently sometimes succeeding in,

Figure 27. A male tarantula on the move in the fall of 2011, a season when males search for receptive females of their species.

converting the male into a meal. End of story for that male. Sexual cannibalism is widespread among the spiders in general, and so it is not too surprising that male tarantulas have to cope with this possibility as they try to pass on their genes to the next generation. But even if a mature, ten-year-old male tarantula survives his interactions with the opposite sex, his days are numbered inasmuch as the end of the mating season usually coincides with senescence and the final stage of his life.

In a species in which males are certain to expire at a particular time, males near the end would seem to have something to gain by encouraging their mate to consume them—provided that the cannibalistic female converts the male's body into more offspring (or offspring that are in better condition), *providing* that the female uses her dead partner's sperm to fertilize the eggs that become those youngsters. In some spiders and mantids, cannibalism is fairly common, and at least in a wolf spider and a funnel-web spider, females that have eaten a male do produce either more or better progeny.

Because the benefits of sexual cannibalism are usually more obvious for hungry females than for consumed males, some persons, notably the famous evolutionist Stephen Jay Gould, dismissed the notion that a male might actually gain descendants by permitting a mate to kill and eat him (after or while transferring sperm to a cannibalistic partner). Gould argued that hypotheses on how males might benefit from participating in schemes of this sort were symptomatic of the tendency of certain of his fellow evolutionary biologists to search for adaptation in places where the search was unnecessary. As far as Gould was concerned, the explanation for sexual cannibalism was clear—females of certain predatory species benefited from the calories and nutrients gained by consuming their mates. Period. No point in asking whether males might also counterintuitively benefit from an event that turned them into a tasty meal for a female.

And it is true that in some cases of sexual cannibalism, males appear to go out of their way to avoid providing females with a terminal, from the male's perspective, feast. Male praying mantises, for example, tend to be exceedingly cautious in their approach to females, as would be expected if the males in question had nothing to gain and much to lose from being captured and eaten by their inamorata. In addition, males of a couple of species, including *Stagmomantis limbata*, are more attracted to well-fed (and therefore presumably less dangerous and more fecund) females in the lab and field than to poorly fed individuals. Moreover, in at least one other study, males were far more attracted to females that had consumed a high-protein diet as opposed to a high-lipid diet, a difference related to the protein requirement imposed on females that are making eggs. In cases of this sort, males appear to distinguish between protein-deprived versus pleasingly fertile females probably on the basis of the pheromones they release. The fact that males avoid the females that would have the most to gain by eating them suggests that when sexual cannibalism does it occur in these species, males lose and females benefit.

Still, even if in some animals sexual cannibalism provides advantages only for females, is this true for every species in which males are some-time devoured by females? Shouldn't each case be examined carefully by researchers willing to do so? The answer to my rhetorical question comes from the Canadian biologist Maydianne Andrade who wondered if male redback spiders boosted their reproductive success by permit-ting, even encouraging, a copulatory partner to polish them off, a fre-quent outcome in matings of this species.

Redbacks are relatives of the black widow spider, which are not uncommon in the Phoenix area, both in town and out in parts of the desert. As is true for this group of spiders, males are tiny in comparison to females and have very little chance of surviving the trip from one web to another in the quest for another mate, should they succeed in copu-lating with one web builder. Thus the cost to a male is small if he com-mits suicide while transferring sperm to a first and only partner, which he can do (and sometime does) by performing a backflip into her jaws, to which the female may respond by biting into her agile sexual com-panion. The reproductive benefit to the male is substantial, as we now know because of research by Andrade; female redbacks that have eaten a partner are much more likely to fertilize their eggs with his sperm than if the male lives to try to find another female. So here is a case of adap-tive sexual suicide by males, a titillating example that is also instructive by showing how useful it is to consider hypotheses on the reproductive value of animal characteristics, no matter how much they seem at first glance to reduce, rather than raise, individual reproductive success.

Another carnivore I encountered during my September excursion along Deer Creek was a handsomely decorated beetle larva endowed with lateral orange spots that contrasted nicely with its chocolate-brown body color. I found and photographed this insect as it wandered over some large rocks near the stream. Initially, I guessed the gorgeous grub might be the larval stage of a firefly (i.e., a lightning beetle in the family Lampyridae) but with the aid of two real entomologists, Ted MacRae and Joe Cicero, I learned that it was the immature form of a soldier beetle (a member of the family Cantharidae). In my defense, the can-tharids and lampyrids do belong to the same superfamily of beetles (the Cantharoidea), and so their larvae can be expected to be at least somewhat similar in appearance and behavior. True to expectation, both firefly larvae and soldier beetle larvae are predatory. Some larval fireflies feed on snails; the nonadult soldier beetle larva that I found near the creek probably hunts, captures, and eats a variety of immature insects found in the leaf litter in which it lives, according to Joe Cicero. (Another member of the genus has an exotic and admirable prey preference for immature ticks that have fed on the blood of their hosts.)

The fact that I have only seen a single soldier beetle larva during my walks along Deer Creek probably stems from the rarity with which larvae leave the shelter of the ground cover that is their home and cafeteria. The adults of the beetle, which Cicero said were almost certainly *Chauliognathus lecontei*, are occasionally abundant here, gathering in groups on flowering plants to mate or at least to try to mate in the case of males. Like their larvae, adults of this species are brightly colored and conspicuous, a sign that they are almost certainly well defended, chemically speaking. In fact, some adult members of the genus *Chauliognathus* are known to have glands that can release unpleasant chemicals should the insect be disturbed by a potential enemy. Interestingly, a 100-million-year-old soldier beetle entombed in Burmese amber had extruded a set of defensive abdominal glands just before it was coated and killed in the tree resin that provided its final resting place. Soldier beetle antipredator mechanisms have evidently been around for a very long time.

One living species, *C. fallax*, acquires the chemicals that it uses for self-defense from the plants on which it feeds; this species, which is warningly colored, has been rejected by potential predators, like birds, lizards, and spiders, in laboratory tests. So at least some soldier beetles have evolved the recycling recipe used by monarch butterflies (and many other unrelated insects, like the moths that feed on vining snapdragons) in order to discourage predators from eating them. The recipe: ingest plant defensive chemicals and then reuse them for self-protection, a presumably less costly way to acquire toxins and the like than assembling the molecules from scratch, an ecological recycling trick that has probably been around for tens of millions of years but one that can still arouse admiration in entomologists and hikers.

Daddy Water Bugs

November 2011

November is a quiet month along Deer Creek. Temperatures have fallen sharply, especially at night, and many of the local plants have responded by shutting down their photosynthetic factories once again. The sycamore leaves are now yellow, and some have fallen from their perches high in trees that have grown substantially over the years following the fire. Likewise, the leaves of the more delicate streamside willows are turning or have already done so; most have adopted a pale yellowish-green hue, although one tree has opted for dark red, a rare exception to the rule that red fall foliage is absent in the canyon here.

But even as most of the perennial plants are becoming dormant for a number of months, the seedlings of next year's flowering annuals have begun to poke up to the surface. I recognize the tiny stork's bills (also known as the red-stem filaree), the nonnative member of the genus *Erodium* that has invaded much of western United States. These will produce their pinkish flowers and then their tiny stork's bill fruits in February or March, if all goes well. But I do not know for sure the name of the very small two-leaved starter plants that have forced their way through the remains of a thin cow pie covering the stony ground by the trail. I suspect that these are one of the lupines of the area, whose seeds have received just enough moisture this late fall to induce them to germinate. Although they will need more rain to make it to maturity, their presence here in November is a good sign. Plants that get started in November have a reasonable chance of making it to the reproductive stage in the early spring of the following year.

On the zoological front, I find a belostomatid water bug male with several dozen big eggs glued to its back floating in the streamlet (figure 28). In these large aquatic insects, females deposit their eggs one by one on the back of a sexual partner. He then takes over, sometimes bobbing up and down at the surface of the water so that the eggs are kept well aerated. Moreover, because these bugs are well armed with a stabbing proboscis, most potential insect egg predators give egg-laden males a wide berth. It is a novel pleasure for me to see one of the world's rare paternal insects in action.

I learned about water bugs after coming to Arizona State University (ASU) in August 1972, when I was told that I would be acquiring a graduate student, Robert L. Smith, from a colleague, Mont Cazier. The

Figure 28. A male giant water bug carrying the eggs of his mate(s) on his back, a behavior that makes these males a rare example of paternal insects.

details of the acquisition are lost in the mists of time, but I was happy to claim Bob as my very first graduate student at ASU. For one thing, he had largely completed his thesis research on belostomatid water bugs, and for another, I could see that his thesis was going to illuminate the lives and evolution of these spectacularly paternal insects. My supervision, such as it was, consisted primarily of praising Bob for his accomplishments.

One of the things that I learned from "my" graduate student was that the parental services of male water bugs like *Abedus herberti* were extremely important to the survival of those big eggs on his back. Egg pads that were removed from their caretakers failed to give rise to baby water bugs. So the parental care provided by male water bugs is essential to the welfare of the young in their charge.

Of course, a $64,000 question surrounding male behavior is, what's in it for them? While they are loaded down with eggs, males do not feed (unencumbered water bugs are ferocious predators capable of stabbing, liquefying, and then ingesting the fluids that arise from the digestion of prey, which can be as large as frogs and fish). While burdened with eggs, the bugs are more conspicuous and so presumably more vulnerable to their own predators, which include very large fish and herons, kingfishers, and the like.

The point is that male water bugs pay a price for their warmhearted caregiving behavior. (Do not take "warmhearted" literally.) Persons with an understanding of natural selection theory, among them Bob Smith, do not expect males of any species to lavish care upon offspring derived from eggs that they had not fertilized. This expectation led Bob to study the mating behavior of *Abedus herberti*. He documented the insistence of male water bugs on copulating with their egg-donating partners before and repeatedly during the period when the female was laying eggs on his back. In this way, the male presumably increased the odds that his sperm, and not those stored within the female from a previous mating, would fertilize the eggs that he was going to be responsible for after the departure of his partner.

In order to test whether there was a risk to paternal males that they might care for offspring other than their own, Bob did an ingenious experiment in which he first mated a female with a male homozygous for a dominant mutation whose developmental effect took the form of a light stripe down the back of the offspring sired by the mutant male. The female, which stored sperm from her mutant male partner in a special sperm storage organ within her reproductive system, was a month later presented to a male that Bob had vasectomized so that he could not supply his mate with sperm. This male copulated normally and frequently with the female, and she laid eggs on his back at intervals between copulations, as is the custom with water bugs. But the only viable offspring that later hatched from this union had stripes down their backs, demonstrating that the female had used some stored sperm from her previous mate to fertilize eggs that were given to another male. Thus, water bug males do run the risk of providing for the offspring of other males if their partners have mated previously before laying eggs on a more recent mate's back.

To examine the effect of mating order on egg fertilizations, Bob sequentially gave virgin females two mates, one of which was the mutant striped form and the other the typical nonstriped male. He could later determine which partner had sired the offspring that hatched from the eggs received by matching the resulting offspring's appearance with that of the two males. As it turned out, the last male's fertilization advantage was overwhelming. If this last male was a mutant striped individual, the offspring he cared for were striped and thus were his own genetic progeny. When the second male to mate was the typical form, then the offspring were not striped, and so this male had fertilized the eggs on his back. In other words, "sperm precedence" (to use the fifty-dollar word invented by reproductive biologists) was essentially 100 percent, with the sperm of the last male sexual partner achieving fertilization precedence over those that the female had received earlier and stored in her spermatheca.

The fact that a single copulation at the start of a male-female interaction was enough to give the last male a complete fertilization advantage posed another puzzle with Bob asking why males insisted on mating after receiving four or so eggs from a partner. Perhaps males that mate repeatedly insure that their sperm are placed in the optimal location from which to fertilize eggs as they are laid; the frequent injections of sperm may push any preexisting sperm away from the site of fertilization, insuring that none of a previous partner's sperm would have a chance to slip into an egg or two.

The competition among males and their sperm appears to have affected a great many features of male behavior and physiology in the animal kingdom. To take just one example, males of an Australian mantis appear to boost the amount of sperm passed to a mate when they have been housed with several other males but only a single female. Under these conditions, males have little to gain reproductively by withholding ejaculate from that female. If she does mate with more than one of the males in the cage, a male that passes on larger quantities of sperm may fertilize a larger fraction of his female's eggs than one that holds back only to fail to find another sexual partner. The course of evolution can depend on which male's sperm win the competition derby.

Mountaintop Snow

December 2011

This is the dormant time of year again, a time when nothing much seems happening in the animal or plant world by Deer Creek. True, a ruby-crowned kinglet flits in among the yellow-leaved willows that line the creek. How this tiny and extremely active bird can manage to make a living at this time of year in such a cold and barren place is astonishing. But kinglets are astonishing creatures capable of dealing with much colder winter temperatures than the ones they encounter in the Mazatzals. Indeed, the even smaller golden-crowned kinglet, a close relative of the ruby-crowned, can survive nighttime temperatures 40 degrees below freezing.

Far above the kinglet and the willows, a dusting of snow decorates the highest parts of the mountains (figure 29). Not only does the snow make for an aesthetic landscape but the slow release of moisture from the higher elevations during the warmer springtime also has profound environmental consequences for the area. The plants growing under and near the water provided by the melting snow are among the primary beneficiaries of a system that gently boosts soil moisture levels without causing the intense runoffs and erosion of the sort that a summer thunderstorm can generate. Snow water that is not quickly absorbed by the soil in spring slips down drainages to canyon bottoms below, where

Figure 29. In winter, the foliage of Deer Creek's recovering willows turns yellow. A light dusting of snow is visible on the distant peak in the photograph.

it rejuvenates creeks and the riparian zone. Willows, sycamores, and a host of other plants benefit from water provided in this fashion. And ditto for the insects and other animals that depend on plant growth for their welfare.

One of the many concerns associated with probable global warming in the Southwest is a reduction in the winter snow pack in the mountains of this part of the world. When the snow pack is low, spring runoff is reduced, and in a water-challenged region, this result worries farmers and city water managers, among others. But is global warming real? Although climate experts usually acknowledge that one cannot be sure that any one feature of modern climatology, such as a reduced snow pack—or the Willow Fire—is the product of global warming, the fact that drought and most of the big fires in Arizona have occurred in the past decade or so makes one wonder if higher temperatures are not at least in part at fault.

The other day I read Paul Krugman, the economist-columnist of the *New York Times*, who asked his readers to think about the possible effects of global warming in producing undesirable events in much the same way that loaded dice generate statistically biased results. In this column, Krugman had apparently adopted the metaphor first offered by James Hansen, the ex-governmental climatologist who has spoken out time and again in a largely fruitless attempt to get policy makers to acknowledge the negative consequences of climate change. The point of Hansen-Krugman's crooked dice analogy is to acknowledge that sure, any one major drought or the Willow Fire may have occurred with or without global warming, but the *odds* of extreme events have been raised by the small but real increase in the average temperatures affecting Arizona (and the rest of the West). An average increase in temperature translates into a greater frequency of extreme temperatures, which promotes a greater likelihood of extreme drought, which in turn is linked to reduced snowfall, all of which makes mountain forests in our state somewhat more vulnerable to a massive wildfire. This view treats the effects of global warming like the difference between playing Russian roulette with a pistol loaded with two bullets versus one (to use another analogy altogether).

At least in the United States, however, some persons refuse to believe that man-made climate change is occurring. Many of the nonbelievers are vehement in their rejection of this possibility. Yet a scientific consensus on the matter has already been achieved—years ago in fact. A major scientific society, the American Association for the Advancement of Science (AAAS), broadcast a statement in 2005 to the effect that "the scientific evidence is clear: global climate change caused by human activities is occurring now, and it is a growing threat to society. . . . The pace of change and the evidence of harm have increased markedly over the last five years. The time to control greenhouse gas emissions is now." And in 2007, the International Panel of Climate Change (IPCC), which has produced lengthy reports authored by leading scientists in the field, concluded that man-made climate change is "very likely," by which they meant that this conclusion was almost certainly right.

But why should we give special credence to the AAAS and IPCC? My good opinion of scientific organizations may well stem from the fact that I am one of the tribe, admittedly a now retired scientist no longer with a professorial position at Arizona State University. But once a scientist, always a scientist. Nonscientists often differ in their enthusiasm for scientific endeavors. Indeed, a considerable fraction of the American public thinks that it is safe to ignore or dismiss or disagree vehemently with the scientific consensus that global warming is real and that humans are responsible. According to a Pew Research Center poll in 2009, only a third of all respondents believed that human activity is responsible for climate change. A more recent public opinion poll revealed a slight increase in that figure: up to a little over 40 percent of respondents are now ready to accept that humans are responsible for global warming—but over 60 percent do not think that a warmer earth will pose a problem for them in their lifetimes, and fewer than 20 percent believe that the president and Congress should make combating climate change a top priority.

Those who flat-out dispute the scientific consensus follow a coterie of politicians, pundits, and skeptics of various sorts. In the political corner, we find, for example, Sarah Palin, the ex-Alaska governor and ex-vice-presidential candidate, writing in the *Washington Post* several years ago, "We can't say with assurance that man's activities cause weather changes." And because we cannot know for sure, we can, Palin believes, afford to do nothing about possible climate change.

In the pundit corner, we have George Will, who opined (also in the *Washington Post* in 2009) that "the data scandal and burying of conflicting opinions [about climate change] that has recently come to light show that this is indeed more a cultish lemming movement than any scientific phenomenon. Let there be no doubt, there is a HUGE amount of money and personal prestige now invested in perpetuating the climate change movement." Will's decidedly negative view of those arguing for action against a warming world is encapsulated in the title of his op-ed piece, "The Climate-Change Travesty."

And don't I have to admit that scientists are prone to fads and willing to engage in safe (i.e., consensus-driven) research as they scamper about trying to secure funding and the academic prestige that comes from acquiring large grants? Yes, I do have to admit these things. Academic success is measured in part by the number of papers one publishes in respectable scientific journals. It is easier to produce papers that conform to the current consensus view than to publish articles demonstrating that the consensus is false. It costs money to do the research that has the potential to be publishable; getting grants is a critical necessity for most scientists, including those working in the area of climate change. Not only is the money necessary to collect the data needed to publish, but young scientists must often demonstrate grant-getting ability if they are to receive tenure and to continue to be employed in universities, both highly desirable outcomes for young, middle-aged, and even older scientists.

Thus, young scientists, and others too, are under great pressure to fund and publish their work, which might lead some researchers to engage in self-deception and others to practice outright fraud. These problems are mitigated, however, because as a general rule, scientists do not rush to form a consensus but instead debate, review, and repeatedly test the claims of their peers. When, in the late 1800s, global warming was first said to be caused by an accumulation of carbon dioxide in the atmosphere, the idea was not widely accepted nor even much discussed for many years. During this period, there was no way to determine whether carbon dioxide, which constitutes only a tiny fraction of the gases in the atmosphere, could absorb enough infrared radiation outbound from the Earth to make a difference to the Earth's climate. Nor was there a means to determine the relative effects of carbon dioxide versus water vapor, another quantitatively small component of the atmosphere with the potential to absorb infrared radiation. Even by the mid-1950s, only rough estimates of the possible climatic effect of carbon dioxide were available.

Nonetheless, in 1956, the climatologist Gilbert Plass published a paper in which he summarized the evidence at hand. On the basis of this review, he predicted that a doubling of carbon dioxide concentration in the atmosphere would generate a large (3.6 degrees Celsius) increase in the Earth's surface temperature. Because it was clear even in 1956 that fossil fuel was being burnt as if there were no tomorrow and, moreover, carbon-releasing deforestation via cutting and burning was rampant, Plass went on the record to claim that humans were significantly increasing the carbon dioxide concentration in the atmosphere.

A year or so after Plass's paper, Charles Keeling began to measure atmospheric carbon dioxide at the top of the Hawaiian volcano Mauna Loa. His work eventually confirmed that the concentration of the gas has been rising steadily year after year, in keeping with the premise that human activity was rapidly altering the makeup of the atmosphere. When Keeling began his work, carbon dioxide composed 315 parts per million in the atmosphere; now the atmosphere that we breathe has topped 400 parts of carbon dioxide per million, a substantial increase in a mere fifty years or so. Well before these data were available, Plass predicted that if human-associated increases in carbon dioxide concentration really were occurring, then researchers would be able to detect an increase in the Earth's average temperature by the year 2000. Many such studies have been completed in the last decade or so, and they consistently show that Plass was right. The match between expectation (i.e., prediction) and data (i.e., actual evidence) is such that a consensus gradually formed within the climatological community that, yes, the world's climate is changing and not for the better.

The power of this approach should be pretty obvious. On the global warming issue, for example, Plass and others have used carbon dioxide theory to make formal predictions that could be and were checked against data collected *after* the predictions were spelled out. If these predictions had been shown to be incorrect, the scientific community of climatologists would have remained highly skeptical, if not downright dismissive, of the idea that carbon dioxide concentrations and global warming were related phenomena. But because the evidence was what it was, scientists now generally take the connection very seriously.

This case illustrates that first and foremost a scientific consensus on an issue is achieved by repeatedly *testing* the proposition in question. The process appears to have worked well not because scientists are saints dedicated purely to the disinterested acquisition of knowledge for knowledge's sake but because scientists critically review the ideas of their colleagues. Judgments by others determine whether a particular research manuscript ever sees the light of day. Should a manuscript become a published research article, the conclusions presented there may continue to be examined by skeptical scientists because of the benefits of demonstrating in print that so-and-so's idea is wrong after all. Science really is capable of self-correction, again not because scientists are selfless but precisely because scientists are competitive self-promoters who strive for high social status in the community of their peers.

At the same time, if you were to press any scientist, no matter how convinced of the reality of global warming, that person would probably admit to a small, all right, a very small, but still measureable, amount of residual uncertainty. Scientists usually acknowledge, albeit somewhat grudgingly, that no tested theory or hypothesis can be considered right or wrong with absolute and complete certainty, because new tests could conceivably change the established view. After all, this is exactly what happened with respect to the carbon dioxide theory of global warming.

Outside observers who fail to appreciate or understand the hypothetico-deductive method, sometimes because they do not want to understand the approach, often urge the public to withhold judgment on an issue, like global warming, on the grounds that more research is needed or because some scientific experts have not accepted a hypothesis that many others have agreed is almost certainly true. But although scientific skeptics serve a useful purpose by continuing to consider and test alternative hypotheses, I think it makes sense for the rest of us to accept the consensus scientific view, if one exists. A position backed by a large number of independent, competitive researchers deserves our respect. These specialist researchers understand the field in which they work and are familiar with the findings of other similar experts. They are in a far better position to analyze the validity of the conclusions reached by their fellow specialists than any of us outside the field. So if a large proportion of all academic climatologists agree that humans are contributing to global warming, as indicated by the reports of the AAAS and IPCC, then one can argue, as I have, that their conclusion should be given more weight by the rest of us than the counterview of a small minority of fellow scientists in opposition. As for nonscientific skeptics and opponents, their positions can generally be ignored, no matter how appealing their politics or punditry.

Yes, there is a chance that a majority of true experts are wrong on a given subject, but there is also abundant evidence that modern scientific consensuses are usually correct. This evidence takes the form of cars that use less and less energy to get from A to B, light switches that work, cornfields that produce more corn than ever, computers that do what they are supposed to do, medical procedures and drugs that cure illnesses, and so on. Almost every aspect of modern life from agriculture to zoo management is based on scientific research. True, in some academic circles people argue that science is just one of many equally good ways to discover the truth about the natural world. But, as Richard Dawkins has pointed out, if the advocates of this view are ever found in airplanes 33,000 feet up in the air, then they are complete and utter hypocrites. Because science works, airplanes fly; scientific consensuses are not arbitrary; and thus, there is good reason to accept current scientific opinions held by a large majority of scientific specialists as the best available, albeit never perfect, basis on which to develop social policy.

If global warming is truly global and if it will grow ever more intense, its current effects on Deer Creek will be dwarfed by the consequences of a changing atmosphere. For example, even now in the mountains of

Switzerland where reliable snow cover is a critical ingredient for attracting winter visitors, the future looks bleak for those dependent upon this kind of tourism. On a much larger scale, shorter periods of snow cover in all the mountains of the world, and in the high latitudes as well, will affect not just water runoff and winter tourism but also the soil temperature, the livelihood of plants and animals that have evolved under the current climatic regime, and most worryingly, the global patterns of air and water movement that control the whole world's climate. We can already see more than the outlines of this problem in the arctic, where rising temperatures have led to an ever-greater loss of the summer ice pack. The replacement of reflective snow and ice with dark, heat-absorbing ocean water leads to a positive feedback cycle as the water takes up more solar radiation and becomes warmer, which produces more ice melt with the potential to alter oceanic and atmospheric currents far from the arctic itself.

It is enough to make one thoroughly glum, but at least we do not have to find shelter at night in snow-covered pines in the manner of kinglets. The absence of a blanket of snow on some nights due to global climate change could conceivably make it difficult for these little birds to survive. OK, I am speculating. But even if true, it merely gives us one more small reason to worry about the climate changing when we already have more than enough cause to be concerned.

"Spring" Is Here

January 2012

I n the early morning, the shadows are pronounced on the north-facing slopes and there is still a slightly wintry feel to the Mazatzals. However, temperatures are on the rise. I do not know to what extent global warming is altering the cycle of the seasons in this part of the world. But it is noticeable that the plants along Deer Creek, or some of them, are already beginning to respond as if spring is at hand. Although the willows are now essentially leafless, the annual lupines are leafing out, producing their attractive arrays of tear-shaped, hairy-edged leaves as a preliminary to additional growth and flowering. The same is true for the perennial blue dicks, which have sent up their smooth, thin, oniony leaves from underground corms. Eventually, the plant will produce a long stalk adorned on the top with a tight cluster of attractive blue or purple flowers, but today, the flowering of the plant has to be anticipated rather than experienced (figure 30). Still, just to know that the flowers of blue dicks are on their way tells me that spring is coming.

No waiting is necessary to observe and appreciate the miniature white lanterns that make up the flowers of the manzanitas, a good-looking plant even when not in flower thanks to its smooth, red-brown trunks and its pointed leaves, which are edged in a barely visible line of yellow.

Figure 30. In January, the elongate leaves of Papago onions may already have formed from underground corms of this plant.

The species under observation, the pointleaf manzanita, is common in the interior chaparral of Arizona and Mexico in general and along Deer Creek in particular. The flowers give rise to small green fruits that turn red then brown as they mature. The seeds within germinate best when exposed to smoke and water that has passed through charcoal. In other words, here is a fire-adapted species, one of many that constitute the chaparral in the foothills of Arizonan mountains, a habitat type that is highly flammable, as was demonstrated emphatically during the massive Willow Fire in 2004.

Another even more conspicuous fire-adapted component of the Deer Creek chaparral is provided by the shrub live oaks. Although the fire reduced the aboveground portion of the oak to ash and charcoal, the substantial belowground component remained alive in many cases because the tree produces a very deep, fire-resistant set of roots and rhizomes. From the root crowns come new plants, which as they get larger invest in additional root material that moves outward and from which come still more little oaks, creating a clone that can cover a large area. Judging from the wealth of three- or four-foot-tall oaks in the once-burnt areas in the lower parts of the Mazatzals, this species can rebound from even a devastating wildfire in less than a decade.

The oak is one of those plant species in which individuals produce both pollen-producing male flowers (short, droopy catkins) and acorn-producing female flowers (the flowers are inconspicuous structures that appear from a twig at the base of a leaf or leaves). Whether the oaks invest in making their modest flowers in spring probably depends on the amount of rain that has fallen during the preceding winter months. This year appears to have been a discouraging one for sexual reproduction by the local oaks, but the "trees" themselves are here to stay, and perhaps some individuals may spread by asexual reproduction despite having given up on sexual reproduction via acorns this year. The manzanitas (or some of them) are putting their money on their flowers and fruits, although here, too, there are extreme drought years when the crop of "little apples" produced by these plants is small to nonexistent. You have to know when to fold them if you are a plant growing in an arid place; evolutionary processes have endowed the long-lived shrubs here with that very valuable knowledge.

The Creek Is Running

February 2012

T he stream is as full of water as it ever is in late winter and early spring. The water in the creek is clear as it runs downhill to the east (figure 31). Once more, it looks as if a hiker could drink deeply from the stream, but at this time of year, thirst really is not a problem. The relatively cool weather, the crisp air, and the pleasant noise of the running creek all combine to make a walk into the Mazatzals a comfortable proposition without fear of dehydration.

The plants of the area have grown substantially even in the short period between my visits. The first of the blue dicks are in flower, waving their cluster of three or four waxy blooms from the top of narrow stems ten inches or so tall. At the base of the ovaries of these flowers are six nectaries, secretory glands that provide nectar to reward pollinators for visiting the pretty flowers. Floral nectaries of this sort are of course widespread in plants as they compete to attract insect visitors and the like to their flowers where the visitors may provide pollination services for the plants.

Interestingly, many plants also produce *extrafloral* nectaries at sites well away from their flowers. These sugar-secreting devices primarily induce ants to take up residence in the plant where they inadvertently provide protective services by deterring herbivores that would

Figure 31. Rain or snowmelt has recharged Deer Creek sufficiently so that miniwaterfalls have formed along the water course.

otherwise strip the plant of its leaves or other useful tissues. The barrel cacti of the Sonoran Desert to the south provide a prime example of this sort of thing, with the plant investing in small nectar-secreting organs near some of its spines; ants come searching for the sugary rewards provided by these extrafloral nectaries and are presumed to help the cactus remain free of cactus-consuming insects. In fact, research on barrel cacti has shown that by giving ants carbohydrate rewards, the plants make these little omnivores hungrier for the nitrogen-rich herbivores that eat cactus flesh if left to their own devices. Ants need a balanced diet, apparently, and the only way they can get it while living on barrel cacti is to be on the alert for edible herbivores that come to the cactus with the goal of taking bites out of the plant.

The lupines along the creek have marched ahead developmentally like the blue dicks so that plants with only leaves a few weeks earlier now have flower stalks with blue and white blossoms lined up from bottom to top. There are even a few Mexican poppies with their exuberant orange flowers that are beginning to open up this morning in response to the gradual warming of the day. The much smaller but still attractive flowers of a native pea belonging to the genus *Lotus* are open and will remain available to pollinators from daybreak to nightfall.

One moderately uncommon plant that is in flower now is the Nevada biscuitroot, a species with white flowers with red-topped stamens that are arranged in little plates or umbels at the top of the plant. A relative of the domesticated carrot and Queen Anne's lace of the eastern United States, this much smaller species reaches a size more consonant with the near-desert and desert conditions in which it lives. Nevada biscuitroot has a vaguely carrot-like taproot that is supposedly edible (as suggested by its common name), and the tuber was in fact eaten by some Native Americans long ago in the western United States. As is typical for most plants, even edible ones, few modern studies have been conducted on this species, although I did find an article detailing the response of the biscuitroot to prescribed burns. This plant flowers earlier and more enthusiastically after such a fire, which presumably reduces competition for soil nutrients while enriching the soil with ash and charcoal. However, most of the other plants examined in this study either did not respond positively to wildfire or actually were less reproductively successful afterwards.

The effects of fire on plant communities are clearly not uniform, as can be seen in the failure of the junipers in and around Deer Creek to get started again. Instead, the burnt trees are still standing, leafless and dead as doornails. Perhaps they will require decades to recover from the effects of the Willow Fire, with seedlings inching out ever so slowly from the remnant patches of surviving junipers. Or else junipers are simply one of those plants that occur only in places that are free from fire for generations. Each plant species has its own evolutionary response to the probability of being burnt, which makes sense given the floral biodiversity of Deer Creek and the various habitats available here.

So Much for Spring

April 2012

Spring does not last forever along Deer Creek. The several species of lupines that began to leaf out in January of this year are now largely finished flowering. Their plump, elongate, soybean-like fruits are lined up along flower stalks in place of the flowers that gave rise to them. The fruits are green now but will turn pale brown shortly before opening and spilling their seeds onto the ground. Likewise, the early flowering manzanitas have moved on to the fruiting stage with little green fruits also scheduled to turn color soon (figure 32). The bears of the Mazatzals, assuming that some have moved into the mountains after the fire, will harvest the manzanita berries and deposit partially digested plant remains in pale, circular bear pies on the trails through the mountains.

I do not monitor the higher reaches of the trail today but instead focus on the approaches to the canyon and the lower portions of the stream. On my way, I enjoy the staghorn cacti with their flashy orange-brown flowers. The large, soft petals of these flowers contrast sharply with the thin spiny stems on which they perch.

Scattered over the pasture, the winding mariposa lilies provide more evidence that spring is not quite over yet. Just as was the case about a year ago, the lilies have grown skinny foot-long stalks to support largely white flowers with touches of purple, red, and yellow. But many of the

Figure 32. By April, spring is so far advanced that many plants, like the mazanita, have already produced their fruits.

lilies have had their day in the sun; their flower petals are now twisted and turned in on themselves rather than fresh and open. Native Americans are said to have eaten the edible bulbs of this and some closely related species. I suspect that most Native Americans were extremely hungry most of the time.

Up along the creek, the barestem larkspurs are attempting to reproduce by flowering exuberantly. This widespread and decidedly inedible plant occurs in almost all parts of Arizona, where it entertains passersby with its gorgeous dark-blue and white flowers. A study of other species of *Delphinium*, of which there are hundreds worldwide, has shown that the prominent spur projecting behind the flower contains two smaller internal spurs in which are found the nectar rewards for a pollinator (figure 33). In the case of larkspurs, bumblebees are the primary agents of pollination. In order to remove the nectar present in the internal spurs, a bee must first insert its tongue into one of the two spurs within

Figure 33. The aesthetic flowers of barestem larkspurs feature elongate projections in which the plant sequesters the nectar that it uses to
reward pollinators for visiting its flowers. When insects try to remove
the nectar, they come in contact with the plant's anthers and so may
acquire pollen for transport to another larkspur.

a spur; after removing whatever nectar it can from that device, it then
must withdraw its proboscis from spur A before inserting said proboscis into spur B. These moves require the bee to shift its position at the
entrance to the flower, a factor that promotes the collection of pollen
from the visited plant, a prerequisite for the later transfer of its gametes
to another delphinium.

The abundance of lupines, lilies, and larkspurs (as well as other plants) is no doubt responsible for the presence of a great many insects, of which the butterflies are a prominent component. I am particularly taken by two species that are active today, one a small brown hairstreak with almost uniformly brown underwings minus the characteristic "tails" that project from the hind wings of most of its relatives. This species, the brown elfin, has a very wide distribution, according to BugGuide.net; the species occupies the eastern states through the mountain west up to Alaska and down into Baja California. Although I am happy to see it and attempt a photograph, my fellow entomologists have apparently almost universally ignored this small and modestly attired species. The one paper on elfins that I find was published in the *Great Lakes Entomologist*, not the most widely read scientific journal.

On the other hand, BugGuide.net does provide the intriguing information that the species was named *Callophrys augustinus* after an Inuit who had been given the European name Augustus by the explorers whom he assisted in the nineteenth century. His real name was supposedly Tattanoeuck. Among the Europeans whom he helped was Sir John Franklin during several of his early expeditions to the Canadian Arctic. Franklin is best known for his disastrous final expedition that began in 1845 and ended in the loss of his icebound ship and all on board after a prolonged and grisly period of starvation, lead poisoning, and scurvy. Augustus did not participate in this last voyage but disappeared much earlier while traveling overland in the 1830s to meet another English explorer, a Sir George Back, according to the *Canadian Encyclopedia*. There we read that "it is not known how he [Tattanoeuck] died." But the heroically helpful Inuit is immortalized, if that is the right word, by having the brown elfin named after him, not that many people know of the connection between the butterfly and the man whose Anglicized name provided an inspiration for the taxonomist responsible for *C. augustinus*.

Although the brown elfin is not a particularly rare insect in the Mazatzals, I encounter a yucca giant skipper for the first time here or anywhere else. This butterfly features very large size (for a member of the skipper family Hesperiidae) and a striking black, grey, and white color pattern. Although apparently not a common species throughout its range, the yucca giant skipper does occur all the way across the southern United States, wherever yuccas are available for its larvae. But yuccas are not at all abundant along Deer Creek, which suggests to me that I have found a wanderer of some sort, perhaps a male that will move on shortly in search of yuccas, a mate-location site for males that wait nearby for arriving females intent on laying their eggs on these plants.

As is true for the far less conspicuous brown elfin, the yucca giant skipper, despite its impressive dimensions and attractive appearance, has not garnered much attention from lepidopterists, judging from the fact that the Web of Science identifies just one paper that deals with *Megathymus yuccae*. This paper outlines the relationship between oviposition decisions by females of the skipper in relation to the size of the yuccas available to them in northern Florida. As it turns out, females lay their eggs preferentially on taller yuccas rather than on fire-damaged plants. The decisions made by egg-laying females, however, do not necessarily translate into higher survival for their offspring, contrary to evolutionary expectation, which is that females should deposit their eggs on the better plants (with "better" meaning "better for offspring survival or size"). I have the feeling that the yucca giant skipper deserves more committed researchers before we can close the book on this issue, but at least we have a start now.

Another first for me is the discovery of a group of mourning cloak larvae clustered together on a willow growing next to the flowing stream (figure 34). Seven closely packed, black, spiny caterpillars encircle a stem of the willow where they have been eating willow leaves avidly. Each inch-and-a-half-long caterpillar has a row of red dots lined up on its back. Creatures that are this conspicuous presumably are chemically protected—but I can find no reference in the scientific literature that confirms or disconfirms my suspicion. If the larvae are in fact distasteful, then even if a bird attacked and killed, and then rejected, one member of a group, the others would benefit from the learning experience their companion provided. The dead individual would also benefit indirectly if, as seems surely the case for mourning cloak larvae, aggregations are composed of siblings, so that if one sib died at the beak of a predator but helped his brothers and sisters survive, then that dead sib

Figure 34. Why do the caterpillars of the mourning cloak butterfly form tight aggregations of individuals that feed together on willow leaves?

would have made an indirect genetic contribution to the next generation. In this way, the genetic basis for forming aggregations of relatives could be maintained in mourning cloak populations.

But if mourning cloak caterpillars are not distasteful, despite their appearance, perhaps there is another adaptive reason for their group-forming habit. One possibility was advanced years ago by Niko Tinbergen, the great animal behaviorist, who speculated that by assembling in conspicuous groups, the larvae of this species (known as the Camberwell beauty in Europe) might intimidate some birds that would otherwise attack and eat isolated caterpillars. This hypothesis suggests that all the members of a group are better protected by moving about the food plant in a tight pack than if they were to go their separate ways. Because mourning cloak butterflies are quite common and very broadly distributed, surely someone will sooner or later try to sort out the various tentative explanations for the fondness that the caterpillars exhibit for other members of their families. May that someone show up soon.

An Illegal Hike?

July 2012

I am off to Deer Creek on a sultry, overcast July morning with the temperature hanging right at 90 degrees Fahrenheit upon my departure from Tempe, despite the earliness of the hour. The clouds overhead prevented even a minimal amount of radiational cooling last night. On the plus side, as long as the clouds persist, the thermometer will not rise as quickly as usual. And in fact, when I arrive at the turnoff to the parking area by the trailhead, the temperature at this somewhat higher elevation must be about 80, a downright pleasant figure comparatively speaking.

I am less enthusiastic about the discovery that a gate blocks access to the trailhead parking area. From a variety of sources, I had the impression that the earlier fire restrictions had been lifted, which should have led to the opening of the gates that had been shut to close off trails all along the Beeline Highway north to Payson. Given the number of people seeking recreational opportunity in the mountains and the recent history of fire calamities, I understand the need to restrict access to the forests and mountains of Arizona—in the period before the monsoon arrives. However, the monsoon has shown up on schedule, and although monsoonal thunderstorms have been relatively few, the showers and higher humidities that came with the season should have been sufficient to keep our public lands from going up in flames. But here is the gate still stretched out across the side road and locked to boot.

On the other hand, I did not see the yellow tape and large No Entry sign that had been here a few weeks earlier when I decided to turn around and head back to Tempe without setting foot outside the car. This morning I convinced myself that if the Forest Service had removed the tape and forbidding signage, they must not care if I parked in front of the gate and walked over to the nearby trailhead. At least, that is what went through my head as I pulled the car over to the side of the road, retrieved my backpack and camera, and marched around the gate. A few hundred feet farther on, I reached the trailhead and began my hike.

True, I could envision returning to find that my car had been ticketed. Perhaps there might even be a forest service crew in a green truck waiting to remonstrate with me about my failure to acknowledge the locked gate. Conceivably (albeit not very conceivably), they might be there with handcuffs and an arrest warrant. I kept on walking. It had obviously rained on the area not too long ago, and the morning humidity was palpable. A pyromaniac I am not. And even if I were, I almost certainly would have been unable to start a fire under these conditions.

The past rain or rains had been well received by the chaparral oaks, the mesquites, the streamside sycamores, the spiny mimosas, and all the other plants growing along Deer Creek. Very little was in flower, but the revived greenery was refreshing. And not just for me and the plant kingdom. About thirty minutes up the trail, I startled a group of seven elk, all does and calves, that left the stream bed at a trot, maintaining their alarmed pace up the long, sloping hillside on the other side of the creek.

The local elk offer yet another example of the manipulation of the environment by *Homo sapiens*. By the turn of the century, the elk native to Arizona had been extirpated by hunters. So in 1913, the Elk Society arranged for eighty-three elk from Yellowstone to be transplanted to the White Mountains of Arizona, where they and later released animals did well, eventually producing a current population of about 35,000 that live in the north central portions of the state. In the summer, elk typically stay in mountains at 7,000 feet or more. But my little band was here at Deer Creek at less than 4,000 feet elevation in late July! Perhaps there are too many elk in the north, especially given the statewide drought, which may have sent hungry animals wandering far afield.

Over the years, Arizona Game and Fish has tried to control the elk population at a level that keeps the cattle growers of north central Arizona happy while also satisfying the elk hunters of our state. Men and women holding elk permits have dispatched more than 11,000 animals in some years, an indication of how numerous these nonnative creatures have become.

After my brief encounter with the elk, I continued walking along the trail as it paralleled the stream course, all of it dry in these lower reaches. Even though large mammals were scarce, there were still things to see, the red fruit of the prickly pears lined up on top of round cactus pads, the presumptive nests (silver dollar–sized fans of excavated dirt) made by harvester ant queens that flew, mated, and then found a damp spot in which to burrow some weeks ago, a large black ground beetle with carnivorous pincer-shaped jaws (an insect I cannot recall ever seeing on earlier walks along the south fork of the creek), and at least two species of buprestid beetles on an assortment of small blue morning glory flowers. The beetles with their Hohokam color patterns had been nibbling the flowers on which they perched; here and there, a pair used the flowers as a mating platform as well.

The sun tried to creep out from the clouds. Sweat beaded on my arms and slid down between my fingers.

Finally, well up the south fork of Deer Creek, I find a few stagnant, isolated pools of water, and then a little farther on a stretch where a six-inch-wide rivulet of water runs downhill to a shallow "pond," home to a good stand of cattails. A water bug swam out from the side of the pond and dove down to hide beneath or within a clump of submerged vegetation off to the side away from the cattails. A big blue-eyed darner dragonfly zoomed downstream before turning around to return up the creeklet in the rapid bouncing flight of this species. I sat on the rocks and ate a half banana and an oatmeal bar before taking a large swig from my water bottle, which also supplied me with a welcome splash of water for my overheated face.

Figure 35. The black-necked garter snake inhabits the creek and surrounding areas where it feeds on canyon tree frog tadpoles.

Before heading back down the trail, I disturbed a very small black-necked garter snake, an aquatic member of this widespread group and a handsome little reptile (figure 35). Probably an immature animal, it quickly entered a small pool of water on the barren rocks near the rivulet. The snake searched rather desperately for a place on the bottom of the little pocket of water where it might burrow into the mud in order to hide from me. The mud, however, was too shallow for this purpose, and so the snake eventually swam up to the edge of the depression and poked its head out of the water. I left it alone, doubtless much to its relief. In my absence, the snake would probably try to capture whatever small aquatic creature had the misfortunate to share its watery world. In my experience, it is not common to find snakes with prey, but once I did see an adult black-necked garter snake in a stream with a plump tadpole in its mouth. I did not envy the tadpole.

Walking back to the car, I fell into the rhythm that steady movement provides, my walking stick swinging by my side with every other step. Beside the trail along the wetter part of the creek were willows that had grown ten and twelve feet tall since the 2004 wildfire. I marched past a large, reddish millipede curled up tightly in the trail in the defensive posture assumed by this creature, which possesses glands capable of secreting unpleasant chemicals. These common and widespread animals feed on the bark of desert bushes and assorted detritus that they encounter on the ground. They are known as the desert millipede (*Orthoporus ornatus*) but Ken, the Bug Guy, offers them for sale as giant Texas millipedes on the Internet at twelve dollars a specimen. I do not collect or photograph the millipede but carry on.

Elk droppings litter the ground in places like licorice jelly beans. But I have never been fond of licorice, so instead of consuming the pellets, I practice what I might say to the forest service personnel at the locked gate, should they be waiting for me. Happily, they are not there. But my car is.

Another Illegal Hike?

August 2012

On the drive up to Deer Creek, I encounter low clouds of a monsoonal nature, but they clear off as I approach the Mazatzals, leaving me and the high desert slightly disappointed because a walk in light rain would have been novel and noteworthy. But now, full sunshine reigns as I approach the trailhead parking area, which continues to be blocked thanks to the gate across the access road. Someone from the Forest Service has replaced the fallen sign telling us to stay out with a new one that also tells us to stay out, an order directed at hikers, bikers, horseback riders, ATV owners, shooters, and everyone else. According to the new sign, the area is completely closed due to extreme fire danger. One of the sign's panels shows an icon of a hiker and walking stick with a red diagonal slashed across the image. The meaning of it all could not be clearer.

Despite the forcefulness of the USFS message, I park the car on the side of the road in front of the gate before heading off to the nearby trailhead. It obviously rained here recently, not a lot but some, probably last night or early this morning. The soil is damp; the humidity is the only thing that is extreme at the moment. Almost immediately, I am soaked with sweat. I could not start a brush fire if I had a gallon of gasoline and a match.

I do not have a gallon of gasoline. Instead, all I want to do is to check out the main fork of Deer Creek, which I have not visited for years. This choice requires that I ignore the USFS warning as I walk past the south fork of the creek before reaching the main branch of the stream, dry as a bone at this time of year. The persistent noise of the highway traffic stays with me until I drop down into the creek bottom and then head due west along Deer Creek proper. As I walk, I imagine again what I might say to any forest service employee who wishes to arrest or rebuke me as a scofflaw who flaunts forest service rules and regulations.

My attention soon switches from rehearsing my plea for clemency to the plants that have responded to the monsoon, weak though it apparently has been. In the creek bed, a host of camphor weed stalks are one to two feet tall but have not yet produced their yellow flowers. Their leaves, however, are as sticky and aromatic (when crushed) as ever. Much less abundant are the sacred daturas, some forming mounds of dark green leaves several feet across. It appears that I have come to Deer Creek a little early to enjoy the daturas to the fullest because the plants are not blooming and instead have only managed to produce a multitude of one- to three-inch blue-grey buds. In a week or so, showy white datura flowers will decorate the stony creek bed.

By the same token, the devil's claws have grown to the bud stage, but except for one plant with an immature, unopened bud, I cannot find any of these big-leaved plants in flower, let alone any endowed with the strange devilishly shaped fruits that the plant's flowers will eventually become. These weird fruits, when dry, have two long, curled horns that presumably hook around the leg of a passing animal and so can be carted off to a new location where the seeds of the parent plant may eventually germinate away from the competition.

For a time I entertain the notion that the devil's claws along the trail belong to a species, *Ibicella lutea*, that is native to South America but is now widely distributed in arid California and even in the drier parts of Australia. Subsequently, as I study SEINet, an Internet resource with a large image library of Arizonan plants, I realize that, no, the plants I had seen must be an Arizonan native, *Proboscidea althaeifolia*. This species and several others in the genus *Proboscidea* have been assigned to the Martyniaceae, or for those of you who find the English language more manageable, the unicorn-plant family. I presume the unicorn label comes from the fruit in its green stage, when the two elongate "fingers" that form the claw in the mature fruit are still pressed together and so look rather like a single horn of the sort a green unicorn might possess. Apparently, the young fruit are edible in an okra-like way, as befits their appearance at this stage. Although I once collected some of these to test their edibility, I never actually carried out the test, in part because of the unpleasant odors associated with them. The repellent smell is said to arise from the glandular hairs on unicorn plant stems. The odorous, sticky substances secreted by these hairs attract and trap insects on occasion, but the plant does not absorb the nutrients contained by the insects it lures to their doom. Apparently, the insect-trapping effect of the hairs is merely a side effect of a trait that has evolved because it kills or repels some herbivorous enemies.

The fruits of *Ibicella* and *Proboscidea* look remarkably alike, so much so that plants in both genera have received the common name "devil's claw." However, species of *Ibicella* have now been placed in a family of their own, the Pedaliaceae. Surely the similarities in appearance between the two genera reflect the evolutionary effects of having a fairly recent common ancestor. If true, the two families should be closely related. However, I have been told that the DNA data are equivocal on this point. On the other hand, it appears that a student of the different devil's claws is convinced that the two families have indeed split off only recently in geologic time. I accept the opinion of this student.

The regenerating sycamores along the creek, and there are hundreds of them, are now in the thirty-foot-tall range, perhaps taller in some cases (figure 36). The burnt trunks of the old trees have begun to fall, but in some cases, the cylindrical trunk of the dead tree still stands like a grave marker that rises in the middle of an encircling fringe of saplings derived from the root ball of the partially deceased tree. Two blue grosbeaks are using the dead outer branches of these old, leafless sycamores as song perches. I find no warblers, however, a disappointment because

Figure 36. The streamside sycamores in and on the edge of Deer Creek have made a remarkable recovery in the eight years since the Willow Fire burned the whole area to a crisp.

migrant warblers should now be coming through along with the blue grosbeaks. A few Bell's vireos still crank out their odd songs from the low vegetation by the creek.

Before the trail begins to climb steadily upward, a trio of three black-headed grosbeaks slips into a pocket of big oaks still standing on the point of land that separates two drainages, one narrow and the other broad. The heat and the hill ahead tell me that it is time to turn around and head back. Which I do, stopping briefly by the gravesite of David P. Cowan, who was buried near the creek in 1926, having reached his eighties before expiring. The site has a headstone and is fenced off, but I cannot find a word on the Internet about Mr. Cowan's occupation or how he came to be buried far from Highway 87 in this isolated spot. But either he or his kin selected a fine location for a grave.

Now that the sun is far overhead, the grasshoppers of the area have come out to bask in the sunshine and so are far more conspicuous than they were on the way in. As I walk down the trail, fat red-shanked grasshoppers jump up from their sunbathing spots on the ground and lumber off well out of camera range, although eventually one stays put long enough for me to get a photo. At rest, the grasshopper looks as if it possesses the kind of reticulated camouflage suitable for a big game hunter or a member of the military on a covert mission. In flight, the hopper looks as if it is seriously overweight. This species and the even more abundant green bird grasshopper are both widely distributed throughout the western United States. The slimmer green bird grasshopper likes to sit in the little oaks by the trail rather than on the ground in open spots (figure 37a). Is this species feeding on oak leaves? The grasshopper is known to consume the leaves of a diverse selection of woody plants. Does it choose shrub oaks in part or whole because its color matches the color of oak leaves, the better to hide from predatory birds?

Several students of behavior have suggested that the tendency of the green bird grasshopper to remain for long periods on the same plant, unlike some other hungry grasshoppers that shift from one plant to another frequently, has evolved in concert with the benefits of concealment. We can test this hypothesis by checking the prediction that warningly colored grasshoppers, which are protected against predators by the poisons or unpalatable chemicals in their bodies, should move about more freely among patches of different plant species, the better to secure the nutritional benefits of a diverse diet. Studies of grasshoppers in the laboratory have shown that, at least in some cases, individuals that consume a variety of plant species do in fact grow faster than those on a more restricted set of foods.

I suspect that I am overlooking a good many specimens of the green bird grasshopper thanks to the leafy green color pattern of the insect that helps make immobile hoppers difficult to spot—if they are perched on the right background. But if seen and then disturbed, the green bird grasshopper flies away and dives into the concealing shrubbery of the chaparral. In contrast, the oak leaf grasshopper relies so heavily on its camouflage that it often remains sitting on the ground without moving

Figure 37. The greenish grasshopper (a) *Schistocercus shoshone* hides in small oaks and other shrubs on the edge of Deer Creek, whereas (b) the brown oak leaf–mimicking *Tomonotus ferruginosus* sits without moving on the ground, probably imitating fallen oak leaves.

as I maneuver close enough for a decent photograph (figure 37b). The immature nymphs of this species look very much like fallen pale brown oak leaves. The adults are too big to pretend to be a dead leaf, and so instead, they select patches of soil that match their uniform pale red-brown coloration. It is a pleasure to see these insects, each with its special color pattern and method of avoiding detection and capture, even if they tend to make it difficult for me to secure their photographic portraits.

The walk west is marked by many more encounters with grasshoppers. The views from the trail are dominated by scruffy shrubs and elegant sycamores, with an occasional young walnut tree and even a handful of Willow Fire survivors, the really big oaks near the creek, thrown in for good measure. A few other trees that also avoided incineration, including small patches of living junipers, are surrounded by much larger stands of their dead companions. The botanical mosaic on the northern slopes above Deer Creek testifies to the erratic path of the wildfire. Fortunately, the Lazarus-like regrowth of the oaks and other shrubby chaparral plants has provided the wherewithal for a host of grasshoppers to return to the area.

I am happy to report that I did not reignite the chaparral, and so I could, with a clear conscience, walk back to my car, which sat by the roadside unattended by forest service personnel.

Sprangletop Heaven

September 2012

I do not know what aspects of the past year's climate created superb conditions for red and green sprangletops, but these grasses have done remarkably well near the creek during the summer months. Entire hillsides are covered in sprangletops, which crowd around the scattered mesquites and prickly pear cacti. Although green sprangletop comes in for some praise from cattle lovers as an edible grass that livestock find appealing, red sprangletop has been criticized for the damage it does in flooded rice paddies, where it reduces rice production. Research on this species has focused on how to kill the grass. Here on the hillsides, the sprangletops are in the neutral zone. They do not appear to have been grazed, nor do they pose a risk to rice growers. Instead, they can be enjoyed for what they are, namely modest grasses that are making a statement of some sort this year, a statement that is, however, hard for me to read.

More traditionally aesthetic are the morning glories in flower at the end of the summer. They come in patriotic colors today: red, white, and blue. Over the years, I have grown familiar with all these species. They may be on Arizona's unwanted weed list, but even so, they have a place in my heart. My particular favorite is the red star morning glory, a species with small but glorious scarlet flowers (figure 38). The plant has

Figure 38. The red star morning glory has small but elegant flowers and attractive foliage as well.

a curious current distribution with a range that includes much of the eastern United States with an empty stretch before appearing again in Arizona and western Mexico. Oddly, the species appears to have been introduced into Arizona, presumably inadvertently given that, as noted before, morning glories are flora non grata here (see page 61) and the red star has little or no economic value. The limited scientific literature on the species focuses almost exclusively on how to get rid of the plant with an assortment of powerful herbicides. These papers appear in journals with grim titles, such as *Weed Technology* and the *International Journal of Pest Management*. It is true that a number of relatives of the red star are pestilent weeds, as they grow quickly in disturbed soil (such as agricultural fields) and will also invade natural habitats, where they crowd out or completely smother native plant species, a problem in eastern Australia, for example. There the invaders secured their foothold after escaping from Australian gardens where they had been grown for their attractive flowers, a disaster that has happened time and again as we move plants all over the world into places where they should not be.

My hiking companion draws my attention to the somewhat less showy but still handsome flowers of the lugubriously named longflower tubetongue, the title of which highlights its unusually long-tubed white flowers. Here is one of the cadre of plants that produces flowers in the evening to attract long-tongued pollinators, especially hawkmoths, which come swooping in to extract nectar from deep within the flower's elongate corolla. The flowers last less than a day, usually wilting soon after pollination has occurred and night has become day (figure 39).

Another genuinely native plant that I am shown today is called babyslippers. Although it is a violet, the plant is quite unlike the familiar ground-hugging species known to us all thanks to their conspicuously cheerful blue, white, or bright-yellow flowers, depending on the species. The violet in front of me has flowers that are so small that I could be forgiven, and I do forgive myself, for overlooking them altogether. But when I am directed to peer closely at the plant's tiny flowers, I see that one of the petals projects forward from a tiny corolla formed from the other petals. The effect is vaguely violet-like.

The babyslippers before me, which only a nearsighted person (or one with a magnifying glass) could truly admire, belongs to a genus (*Hybanthus*) rather than to *Viola*, which is the taxonomic home of the "typical" violets the flowers of which are much more conspicuous. Although the genus *Hybanthus* is a very large one with members scattered all over the globe, the species that have attracted most scientific attention are either those capable of dealing with soils high in nickel, a substance usually toxic to plants, or those that grow in tropical areas. Some members of the genus have been shown to possess a class of compounds called

Figure 39. A honeysuckle with elongate white flowers that have evolved to attract long-tongued pollinators capable of reaching the nectar at the base of the flower.

cyclotides, some of which act as insecticides that no doubt help the plant deal with its small herbivorous enemies.

The babyslippers growing along Deer Creek have an ability to cope with decidedly nontropical conditions, which I presume makes it a moderately unusual member of the group, one that has reached the northern limit of its distribution here like so many other plant genera and families with tropical origins. Nonetheless, botanists have not paid much attention to the plant, judging from the scarcity of scientific articles that mention the little herb. But now that I have been alerted to its presence and its relationship to more familiar violets, I at least will stop ignoring the plant on my walks along Deer Creek.

Fall in Deer Creek

October 2012

Today is merely warm, not hot, on the South Fork Trail. This is the first day of fall in which the high will not reach 90 degrees Fahrenheit in Tempe, and it will be cooler still, of course, here in the Mazatzals. However, the drought continues in Arizona. In some years, the first winter rain comes to the state in October, but probably not this year since the month thus far has been as dry as a bone and no rain is forecast for ten more days. In response either to the dry weather or to the season of the year, very few plants are in flower, just a couple of species of morning glories, a handful of asters and composites, the desert broom with its abundant fluffy white flowers, and some specimens of sweetbush, growing in the debris deposited by floods in the creek bed after the fire.

Sweetbush specializes in the colonization of disturbed areas, such as roadsides, although an occasionally flood-swept island in or edge of a wash is presumably a more natural location for the plant. This perennial, also known as chuckwalla's delight, is positively humming with insect activity, most of which is provided by a small brownish butterfly, Palmer's metalmark, but also by carpenter bees, syrphid flies, and even a few honey bees. Unlike the herbivorous chuckwallas, which do not live in the Mazatzals, the insects are not interested in gobbling up the small and individually insignificant flowers of sweetbush. Instead, the metalmarks and flies delicately sip nectar from the large bouquet of blossoms available to them.

Not much else is happening on the entomological front, although farther up the trail, I encounter a strange caterpillar being pursued and bitten by harvester ants. After rescuing the creature from its pursuers, I admire the glossy black upper part of its caterpillaresque body, which is adorned with thin yellow bands. The sides and underside of the creature are much more striking, as they are colored a bright blue. As is often the case on my walks, I have come across an animal that I have never seen before. I later learn from my colleague, Ron Rutowski, that the brightly colored larva is an immature moth, the prickly pear borer, *Melitara dentata*. I presume that the caterpillar was searching for a place to pupate when it was set upon by ants. Had it succeeded in pupating and then becoming an adult in the fullness of time, the result would have been a very ordinary-looking pale-brown moth, the very essence of nondescriptiveness.

Members of the genus *Melitara* provide the North American analogues of the far more famous prickly pear borers of South America, which belong to the genus *Cactoblastis*. One species in this group (*Cactoblastis cactorum*) was introduced into Australia, where it led to a dramatic decline in the numbers of prickly pear cacti of various sorts that had invaded that continent thanks to nineteenth-century landowners who imported prickly pears to use as hedges and food for their livestock at times of drought. Early on, however, the cacti began to spread like a cancer, and by the 1920s, the plants had invaded an area the size of Great Britain in northeastern Australia, rendering huge areas useless for agriculture. Attempts to mechanically remove the cactus or poison it with arsenic-laden paints were complete failures. In 1927, the authorities introduced *C. cactorum* to the area despite an earlier failure at establishing the insect as a biocontrol agent. This time, the cactus moth's population took hold and then exploded as their larvae feasted on the superabundant cacti available to them. Within four years, the prickly pear infestation was at an end, a miracle as far as the Queensland farmers and politicians were concerned.

The Australian use of *Cactoblastis cactorum* as a biological control agent of an invasive nonnative plant is one of the few big success stories of this sort, an inspiration for additional cactus control efforts in South Africa and the Caribbean. From these places, the moth has unfortunately now moved into areas where it is not welcome, including Mexico and the southern United States, probably through accidental importation. In its nonnative range, the absence of its own biological controls, such as parasitoids that destroy the larvae, make *C. cactorum* a major threat to cactus-rich ecosystems and agricultural fields of prickly pears grown for their edible pads and fruits. There is now a chance that the moth larva will become another example of the unintended consequences of biocontrol efforts along the lines of the cane toad, which Australians brought from South America to combat insect pests of sugarcane. This was a truly terrible idea, as it turned out, with the toad consuming native frogs with far more enthusiasm than it showed when confronted with bugs that attack sugarcane.

Although there is every reason to be fearful, there are some indications that the invader may not be as devastating as some had feared. Studies of the introduced insect in Florida have shown that native members of the prickly pear genus *Opuntia* often manage to survive attack by the larvae of the nonnative moth and do not appear to be severely damaged by the pest. Moreover, cacti that grow close to others with extrafloral nectaries that attract ants gain some protection from the moth's eggs and larvae. So it could be worse. Nonetheless, Arizonan botanists are nervous about what *C. cactorum* might do to our *Opuntia*-rich Sonoran Desert.

The single *Melitara* larva harassed by ants on the trail by Deer Creek does not appear to be enjoying the slightly lower temperatures and the cooling breeze that swirls down out of the Mazatzals, but I am pleased by these signs of fall as well as by the foliage near the creek. The sycamore leaves have begun to change from dark green to a yellow-green; ditto for the leaves of the canyon grapevines that have tried to smother the streamside plants in places. Most of the willow leaves have also begun to fade as they dangle from the thin trees standing along stretches of stream where water still flows at this dry time of year. One or two willows are cloaked in leaves that have turned red, but they merely provide an exception to the rule that the Deer Creek plants lack the brilliant red and orange foliage that makes October a visual delight in the north temperate forests of New England and southern Canada. It is true that the fragrant sumac has a smattering of attractive dark red and orange leaves but nothing that would make a Vermonter envious.

One can wonder, and many have, why it is that plants with deciduous leaves change color in the fall (figure 40). The chemistry of the change is pretty well understood. Plants have green leaves during the spring and summer because of the abundant amounts of green-reflecting chlorophyll in those leaves, chlorophyll being useful for photosynthesis, which provides the plant with the sugar needed for its growth, reproduction, and survival. When fall comes and the chlorophyll breaks down prior to freezing winter temperatures, this pigment is not replaced by new chlorophyll molecules, and so the other pigments in leaves become dominant, first carotenoids that change leaf color from green to yellow, then anthocyanins that are responsible for turning yellow leaves into orange or red ones.

But why exchange chlorophyll for other pigments? Here things get trickier in the sense that there are many competing evolutionary

Figure 40. The leaves of the willows growing along Deer Creek turn yellow and orange in the fall. Do the plants gain a reproductive advantage as a result?

answers to this question. We start with general agreement that by discarding their leaves, deciduous plants in temperate climates save the energy that would be required to maintain functional photosynthetic factories during freezing weather. So deciduous plants avoid the costs that conifers pay as they invest in their thin needles, keeping them alive and well during winter in cold places. It could be that the bright colors of the maple's autumn leaves are simply a side effect of the program to go dormant during winter, with the plant removing valuable nutrients and other compounds from its old leaves prior to dropping them to the ground. With the components of chlorophyll and other materials essentially available for recycling the next spring, the color of deciduous leaves would then be determined by their expendable pigments, such as the carotenoids that give deciduous plants their attractive fall foliage.

But this by-product hypothesis runs into difficulties when you learn that deciduous plants actually make some leaf pigments (including anthocyanins) when they are also dismantling their chlorophyll and recovering important compounds from their deteriorating leaves. These anthocyanins, which make fall leaves so colorful, cost something to make and maintain, even for a few weeks. Why bother if the goal of the plant is to remove and sequester biochemicals of value from its leaves before discarding these nonphotosynthetic appendages with whatever chemicals they still retain?

One possibility is that the replacement pigments are cheaper than chlorophyll but still help protect the leaf from cold temperature damage so that it can continue to shunt nutrients back to the "mother plant." A similar hypothesis is that the replacement pigments help protect the leaf's chemical machinery from the oxidative damage caused by bright sunshine, particularly at low temperatures, so that the leaves can finish their recycling mission effectively. After all, what pigments do is to absorb light energy of particular wavelengths while reflecting other wavelengths back from where they came. By either absorption or reflectance, a leaf could tackle the problem posed by damaging wavelengths of light, the better to keep the internal biochemistry of its leaves in good working order. The fact that the brightest colored leaves are those exposed most directly to sunlight is congruent with the leaf protection hypothesis.

But the leaves most exposed to sunlight (on the outer portions of a tree or shrub) are also probably those most exposed to herbivores, some of which are still active in the fall. Perhaps then by producing colorful fall leaves, deciduous plants gain a benefit by signaling to herbivores that the owners of those leaves are particularly well defended, a benefit that repays the costs incurred by making and incorporating colorful pigments as antiherbivore messages. The suggestion has been made that a key group of herbivores worth deterring via brightly colored foliage are winged aphids, several species of which fly to temperate zone trees in order to overwinter in cracks and crannies in bark. The next spring, they emerge to draw fluids containing sugars and nutrients from the young green leaves of the plant, which has been dormant during the winter. This hypothesis requires that the aphids in question be able to perceive the intensity of leaf color of potential hosts and to use this information to avoid plants whose fall leaves signal that the plant will be producing especially well-protected young leaves the next spring.

Let's consider, however, yet another hypothesis to account for the avoidance of red leaves by aphids (if, in fact, they do avoid leaves of this sort). The counter to the defense-signal hypothesis is that aphids avoid red leaves because they are senescent and no longer contain nutrients, having already exported them back to the mother plant during the pale-green and pale-yellow leaf phases. By keeping away from red leaves, aphids could focus on leaves colored in ways that inadvertently indicate that they are worth probing for the residual nutrients they contain. For one aphid that specializes on birch trees, the herbivore is attracted to yellow leaves to a greater extent than green leaves, suggesting that this aphid responds to color cues associated with leaves in fall.

But a change in leaf color could have evolved as an adaptive signal from the plant's perspective if red leaves communicate to potentially damaging insects that the leaf is about to fall from the plant, an event that could carry insects on the leaf to the ground where they might die prematurely. If so, a plant with colorful leaves could benefit by encouraging insects with harmful potential to keep off, while herbivorous insects might also gain by avoiding nutritionally suspect leaves that would soon fall to the ground.

Figure 41. The fragrant sumac is one of the few plants growing along the creek the leaves of which turn bright red in the fall.

What seems very clear is that there are far more potential explanations for the fall leaf–color shows in temperate forests than there are definitively tested hypotheses. Indeed, in a recent review, the eleven botanist-authors produced a long list of unanswered questions surrounding the adaptive value of red autumn leaves. They did not bother thinking about the red and orange leaves on the fragrant sumac shrubs growing near Deer Creek (figure 41). Until the day arrives when we can fully understand the fall colors of this plant and others in evolutionary terms, we will have to content ourselves by appreciating fall color on aesthetic grounds alone. This is not hard to do.

The Cold Carpenter Bee

December 2012

The fragrant sumac bushes have lost most of their leaves and no longer provide a cheerful exception to the rule that red-leafed plants
are absent from Deer Creek. Although the weather continues unseasonably warm, still most shrubs and trees have stopped pretending that it
is early autumn. Their leaves have turned a dull or dark brown or have
dropped from the plants that had sustained them. The sycamores have
put photosynthesis behind them for the rest of the year and beyond.
Their curving totem-pole trunks are decorated with limbs on which
are arrayed a host of yellow-brown leaves that provide little in the
way of visual pleasure. Soon they will be on the ground surrounding
their patrons.

Given that the year is well advanced and the past several months have
been without precipitation, I was not counting on there being much in
the way of flowers along the creek. And in keeping with expectation,
today on the first day of December almost all the flowering plants of late
October are no longer bright with blooms. The mounds of sweetbush,
which once possessed small yellow tufted flowers that were swarming
with flies and butterflies five weeks ago, have moved on to the "fruiting"
stage, during which time the plant gradually releases thousands of little
dandelion-like seeds into the air.

But here and there, a flower blossom or two still holds sway, especially in the cooler, shaded recesses along the stream bed. A daisy of sorts (perhaps a species of *Xanthisima*) with thin, feathery foliage sports a host of bright yellow flowers. A minute fly hangs out on one of its flower petals. Similarly, the purple tansyasters of the season are not totally finished but instead remind us of the past with a few of their purple and yellow flowers, still perky in amongst a host of dry, colorless flower heads that long ago went to seed. An Arizona penstemon has invested in one last bouquet of red flowers.

These anomalies, however, are just that, anomalies, so that a hike is required between each episode of flowers, not that the walk is unpleasant. The temperature is perhaps ten degrees above normal, nearly ideal for a human visitor to the creek. The sun shines brightly on us all. The creek even continues to flow, but only when one walks well up into the canyon, although the yellow, sludgy algae lining the barely wet stream bottom have produced a bouquet of unattractive organic odors.

On the way back, with temperatures on the rise, a few insects show up to add to the biodiversity of a (warm) winter's day at Deer Creek. A shrub with leathery leaves is home to a number of small yellow jacket visitors that are inspecting leaves, and even a rock underneath the shrub, with great interest. The fact that the wasps have long antennae suggests that they are males out late in the year to search for females that will become queens capable of founding new colonies of these social insects after the winter is over. But here the odd behavior of the wasps has more in common with a person obsessively searching for a set of lost keys in places already inspected than with male insects intent on finding and copulating with females of their species.

The leaves of the plant are speckled with tiny dots of something that reflects the sunlight when the leaves are viewed at the proper angle. Ah-ha. Honeydew. Perhaps the leaves have been showered with the excreta of aphids feeding on leaves higher in the shrub. If so, turning over leaves in the top of the plant should reveal tiny aphids at work siphoning off nutrient-rich fluids in the leaves for their own benefit. A by-product of their leaf parasitism would be the small shiny dots of sticky honeydew on the leaves below. And yes, there are abundant small

Figure 42. A male yellow jacket wasp feeding on exudates from aphids that are sucking plant juices from this shrub.

green aphids on the undersides of the leaves that they have infested. The wasps are consuming recycled plant phloem, which must retain at least some of the compounds, such as sugar, that the aphids try to remove as the fluid passes through their guts and out the other end (figure 42).

The relative abundance of yellow jackets and other wasps at this time of year coincides with the unusually late appearance of a brownish-black coreid bug, the female of the giant agave bug *Acanthocephela thomasi*, the western member of a small genus of extremely large true bugs. Unlike the males of this species, which have massive, thorny hind legs, females have more delicate appendages. The males of a closely related species and males of some other coreids are known to use their power-ful hind legs to grasp rivals as they compete for access to females. Larger males of *Acanthocephala* have relatively larger hind legs with larger "teeth," which they use when attempting to hold onto the abdomen of an opponent, the better to powerfully squeeze that body part in an effort to encourage the rival to flee.

Figure 43. A female of the coreid bug *Acanthocephela thomasi*, a possible mimic of stinging paper wasps when in flight.

Females do not fight with one another for access to mates. They do not have to since males are so motivated to seek them out. Thus, the smaller, thinner hind legs of female *Acanthocephala* (figure 43). But I notice that when the female flies, it looks to me rather like a paper wasp thanks to the coloration of its abdomen that is exposed when the insect is airborne. By virtue of being active at a time when predators that were once naïve about the result of attacking a wasp are no longer naïve, the bug may gain respect from these now-educated enemies (if I am right about its mimicry). It is true, however, that I can find no mention in the scientific literature of a resemblance between a flying female *A. thomasi* and a flying paper wasp. Perhaps I am deluding myself.

Giant agave bugs make a living by piercing plants (agaves and others) and sucking out the sugary contents thereof. The nymphal stages of coreids of all sorts are usually well endowed with defensive glands that secrete or spray unpleasant chemicals at their enemies, especially ants. Adults also frequently have specialized glands that appear to be defensive in nature, although birds will sometimes eat mature coreids despite their presumably unpleasant chemistry. The species, *A. thomasi*, that is here today has bicolored antennae (orange tips on black basal components) and black and orange fore- and midlegs, orange "feet" on the hind legs, a color pattern of the sort generally considered warning coloration with the function of signaling potential predators to back off because of the distastefulness of the brightly colored insect. Perhaps this bug has a double-barreled defensive system linked to its color pattern so that when at rest potential predators are put off by the visual signal that it will be bad tasting, if not downright toxic; should, however, a female take flight, then her possible mimetic resemblance to a stinging paper wasp might deter other predators, such as flycatchers, from swooping in for the kill.

Many other insects have evolved the ability to mimic well-defended species, such as wasps, thereby deriving protection through deception. Mimicry of stinging wasps and bees is particularly common in the flies but has also evolved in other groups, notably among the buprestid beetles in the genus *Acmeodora*, some of whose members are fairly common flower eaters in the riparian zone of Deer Creek during seasons when their food plants are in bloom. In Florida, two biologists from Cornell saw that several species of *Acmeodora* found there looked very much like wasps—but only when the beetles were flying from plant to plant. In flight, these insects held their wing covers in an entirely different way from that of the typical beetle. Instead of spreading apart the two hard-shelled forewings (also known as *elaters*), the wasp mimics kept the two wing covers together while beating their membranous hind wings as they flew away. The manner in which the beetles held their elaters together maintained the integrity of the wing cover color pattern so as to produce a banded-abdomen look of the sort associated with various wasps.

The similarities between *Acmeodora* buprestids and the coreid (again assuming that it is indeed a wasp mimic in flight) provide a nice example of convergent evolution. These unrelated insects may have converged on a shared solution to the heightened probability of lethal bird attack resulting from their relatively slow flight. By changing their appearance when airborne, these beetles and coreids could encourage keen-eyed birds to give them a pass rather than risk grabbing a wasp armed with a powerful stinger.

The female coreid bug was one of the last insects seen during our December walk. One of the first insects to put in an appearance that day was a large bee, discovered early on when the bee was clinging to a small plant growing in the creek bed. Perhaps because the bee's overnight perch was still in the shade and perhaps because the air in the creek basin was decidedly chilly, the bee was immobilized, unable to move even as his perch was broken off and the insect moved to a sunny spot better suited for insect photography. I guessed that the handsome creature was a male carpenter bee (figure 44). The striking blue eyes of the chilled bee led me to the insect's scientific name—*Xylocopa tabaniformis*—when I Googled "Xylocopa with blue eyes."

I have a special fondness for carpenter bee males as a result of studying the mating behavior of another carpenter bee in Arizona, *X. varipuncta*, sometimes referred to as the valley carpenter bee. This species is common in the Phoenix area, where, in the spring, males leave their natal nests (burrows in wood carefully carved out by their mothers) in the afternoon to hover in treetops and other conspicuous sites on ridges and in dry washes. The hoverers can spend three or more hours at their stations, only leaving to return home to logs in suburban backyards or more natural nest sites in desert trees as dusk comes slipping over the land. While waiting at their hovering stations, some males may be visited by females, which are black instead of the deep orange of the opposite sex. The arrival of a female visitor triggers an odd reaction from the male, which flies quickly to a sprig of vegetation in the plant he has been hovering near. There he repeatedly grabs the leaves growing at the tip of a branch and rubs them with his body. The big female typically hovers nearby, almost certainly smelling and evaluating in some way the pheromonal scents released by the male both before and after his leaf-rubbing performance, scents that humans can also smell. (In fact, I

Figure 44. A carpenter bee, *Xylocopa tabaniformis*, that can barely move in the cold of a December morning along Deer Creek.

have on occasion detected a hovering male well before I saw him thanks to the pleasant floral aromas that he was casting to the winds in an effort to lure a female close enough for the leaf-rubbing phase of courtship.)

Most visiting females are unimpressed and depart during the time while the male is pouncing on the vegetation he has chosen to "mark." However, a minority remains in place and then flies to and lands upon the spot that the male has presumably ornamented with his scent. Only then does the male bee land on her back and copulate briefly before releasing his partner, which flies off with the sperm she has received from her mate. This insect species, then, appears to be one in which choosey females exert complete control over the selection of a copulatory partner, presumably on the basis of the male's odor and/or scent-marking behavior.

Some colleagues and I have spent a great many hours hoping to see males and females of the valley carpenter bee interact only to be disappointed more often than not. On most afternoons, very few males and fewer females show up at the landmarks where males station themselves. And even on those rare warm days each spring when the bees do come out in force, females are more likely to visit and leave than visit and stay for a mating. Still, after all is said and done, I feel that my hours of watching have given me at least a partial idea of what the mating system of the valley carpenter bee is all about, a mating system that resembles that of the much more famous leks of some tropical birds, like birds of paradise, and some game birds, like sage grouse. Lekking animals are those in which females come to places with displaying males where females choose mates carefully from among numerous suitors on the basis of their courtship performances.

But what about the mountain carpenter bee as *X. tabaniformis* is informally known? The cold-immobilized male clinging to a twig in front of me today is not going to be very revealing with respect to his mate-acquisition tactics. But earlier in the year, in April, I did see a single presumptive male of this bee hovering for some minutes next to a standing dead tree trunk next to the creek, the remains of a sycamore killed by the Willow Fire. I tried to photograph the bee with very modest results thanks to its restlessness as it looped about and shifted position every few seconds, but during our brief time together, I had the impression that the male was behaving rather like a third species that is common in Arizona, *X. californica*. During one summer when I was living in the Chiricahua Mountains of southeastern Arizona, I found some males of this species hovering by dead junipers and dead agave stalks in which one could see the nest exits (and entrances) constructed by burrowing females. I assumed that the males in question were staking out positions to wait for the departure of young (receptive) female carpenter bees from the nest or nests within the dead plant close to which the male was hovering. These males appeared on their territories throughout the day rather than coming out only in the late afternoon or early evening. The hovering male of *X. tabaniformis* that I saw in April was in action in the middle of the day, which is more reminiscent of *X. californica* than *X. varipuncta*.

My "research" into the behavior of the mountain carpenter bee ended soon after it had begun on that day in April. The male bee quickly departed, and I could not find an obvious nest exit/entrance in the dead sycamore; in any event, I had reached the turnaround point, and soon I too left the area with only guesses about what male *tabaniformis* might be doing. Surely, I thought, there will be some accounts of the behavior of this bee in the scientific literature.

A search, however, of the Web of Science turned up exactly one paper that dealt with *tabaniformis*, a short report from long ago in a minor entomological journal, the *Pan-Pacific Entomologist*. This paper devoted most of its limited space to X. *californica* with a terminal note on the species of current interest to me, *tabaniformis*, which the author had seen in California. But the references in this article led me to another much more substantial piece on carpenter bees in which there were a few more comments on the behavior of the mountain carpenter bee scattered among a much more detailed account of the taxonomy of the bee. It turns out that the species occurs widely in the southwestern United States as well as in much of Mexico. Different populations have diverged considerably in their appearance, resulting in the description of ten subspecies of X. *tabaniformis*, an unusually high number for an animal of any sort. The behavioral aspects of the various populations were presented very briefly, but the sketchy accounts suggest that in some subspecies, males may be active in securing mates only in the late afternoon, whereas in others, males are active during much of the day. Either this one species is a bee in which multiple mating tactics have evolved or those persons responsible for naming the subspecies have lumped together two separate species into one. Taxonomists always face a challenging task that involves a certain amount of subjectivity. Because no one has looked again at the various "subspecies" of *tabaniformis*, we will, for the time being, accept the work that Lois O'Brien and Paul Hurd published nearly fifty years ago, while trusting that someone new will eventually take an interest in the behavioral diversity exhibited by the males in different populations.

But for my purposes, the main point is that the subspecies of *tabaniformis* that briefly entertained me on Deer Creek in April and again in early December of 2012 has never been studied in even remotely sufficient detail with respect to its mating system (or mating systems). This despite the fact that the bee, which is far from uncommon, occurs over a wide area in North America and Mexico. And despite the fact that the diversity of mating systems within the genus offers comparative entomologists a chance to develop a comprehensive picture of the evolutionary history of mating behavior of the 500 species of *Xylocopa*, a genus with a worldwide distribution. How many times has lekking behavior a la the valley carpenter bee evolved in the genus; what was the probable behavior of the ancestor of the carpenter bees; and how did this pattern morph into the mating systems exhibited by today's carpenter bees? These questions and others can be tackled if one has a clear idea of the evolutionary relationships among the members of a genus (i.e., which species are closely related and which are more distant relatives), relationships that could be matched with details on the behavioral traits that these species currently exhibit. We still have a long ways to go before we can begin to deal with these matters. So many insects—so few behavioral biologists!

The Leafhopper Walk

January 2013

January in the Mazatzals is a quiet month under the best of circumstances, but today is especially low key. There has been rain here a while back, and some seeds of spring annuals have germinated, but the combination of the cold snap of a week ago and a long dry spell after the one good round of rainfall has (probably) kept things subdued. The spring annuals are tiny and the perennials largely dormant except for some of the little oaks, the desert brooms, the barberry shrubs, and a few others. The sycamores are completely leafless and the willows have yet to produce a bud.

In contrast to the lack of excitement on the plant front, the winter sparrows of central Arizona are out in force, hundreds of white-crowned sparrows with a considerable number of Brewer's and black-throated sparrows thrown in for good measure. My attempts to call them closer by psshting are universal failures, with the birds fleeing off through the grassy areas or upslope. Often when there are groups of sparrows, they show some interest in a psshter because (as noted before) the sounds I and my fellow birders produce mimic those of birds attempting to attract others to harass a hawk, owl, or other predator. When psshting works, the sparrows fly closer rather than disappear into the distance. But not today.

On the slope to the south that rises from the creek, a large whitetail rises out of the chaparral and moves uphill as its all-but-hidden owner hurries away from the canyon bottom. It takes a few seconds before I realize that the creature attached to that incongruously large white object is a white-tailed deer, a suitable creature for Deer Creek, but the first deer of any sort that I have seen here. I would have guessed that if I were to see a deer in central Arizona, it would be a mule deer, but a little Internet research reveals that although whitetails are more common in southeastern Arizona, they do occur here and well to the north, indeed as far north as Flagstaff. The individual that caught my attention is either a yearling or a doe. He or she does not linger after coming into an opening in the chaparral before slipping back into the cover of the hillside shrubbery.

The elevation of the large and conspicuous tail of the white-tailed deer has attracted considerable attention from researchers who have concluded that one function of the behavior is to announce to any potential predators in view that the owner of the tail has spotted them and will be difficult to capture. The pursuit-deterrence hypothesis rests on the presumption that alerted prey are indeed hard to bring down and thus a mountain lion (for example) that has seen the white flag of a wary deer will find it advantageous to abort any attack it might have planned. The deer benefits and the predator does too by saving its energy to expend on another more vulnerable victim.

The sun shines on the Mazatzals, which have the barest of snow covers high on the reddish ridgetops to the west. The creek makes an appearance a mile or so into the walk with clear, clean water moving steadily downstream before easing underground closer to the trailhead. Two canyon towhees slip out of a mesquite close to me and fly off to another hiding place farther away. In the unseasonable warmth of the day, a few butterflies have become active, including a small orange pierid, a male of the species, observed in unsuccessful pursuit of a much larger female. She signals her lack of interest in copulation by flying steadily higher and higher, an ascending flight of rejection.

I had hoped to find and photograph the dangling inflorescences of the silk tassel bush that was in full flower in January on a walk here in 2011. The plants are not uncommon along the creek, and they have today begun to produce their elongate buds, one of only a handful of shrubs that have at least started the process of flowering (along with the point-leaf manzanita and sugar sumac). But I can find no plant with full-length silk tassels three or four inches long, only small starter tassels of an inch or less. However, while inspecting the silk tassel bush on the way back to the trailhead, one plant's leaves prove to be home to dozens of small leafhoppers, well under a half inch in length. I would have missed them entirely except that as I searched for buds on the shrub at close range, hordes of leafhoppers burst from the plant and redistributed themselves among the grey-green leaves. By paying attention to the insects rather than to the plant, I discovered that although the little leafhoppers were largely green themselves, their color pattern was actually quite intricate, as it featured lines of dark green and blue on pale green wing covers, a central blob of orange-yellow behind the thorax, and a bright blue head with symmetrically placed black dots (figure 45). Actually, I didn't take in all these elements of its color pattern at once but instead relied on the close up digital image that my camera and I had secured.

Now why should a very small insect go to the trouble to produce a complex and colorful body design? As usual, I turned to the Web of Science to see what, if anything, had been written about this apparently insignificant (but brightly colored) insect. First, however, a name for the bug was essential and once again, Bug Guide came in handy. With the help of this resource and some others, it became clear that the Deer Creek leafhopper was the blue-green sharpshooter, *Graphocephala atropunctata*. Once a name was in place, I could investigate scientific publications that referenced this creature with lively colors and a snappy name as well. To my surprise, I learned that the little leafhopper has received much attention from entomologists. Although small in size, the fact that the sharpshooter acts as a vector for a bacterium that when transferred to grapevines destroys the leaves of these plants (and can kill the grapevines altogether, as well as harming other agriculturally valuable plants) makes *G. atropunctata* a VIB (very important bug). Perhaps the local sharpshooters damage the canyon grapevines that grow along the creek.

In commercial vineyards, sharpshooters unquestionably do nasty things, which is why California grape growers and wine producers fear

Figure 45. The blue-green sharpshooter, a small leafhopper, on a *Garrya* leaf. Although tiny, the leafhopper sports an elaborate color pattern.

this tiny insect and another related sharpshooter species. As a result, entomologists have been invited to study the creature to determine (for example) how many *Xylella fastidiosa* a leafhopper can carry around in its gut in relation to the ability of the insect to infect a grapevine upon which it is feeding. (Leafhoppers stab the plant with their sharp proboscis, enabling bacteria to travel into the afflicted plant while the insects secure fluids and nutrients from the host.) The California Department of Food and Agriculture has used this and other basic research findings to develop a major program to combat the vectors of Pierce's disease.

When it comes to analyzing the color patterns of the blue-green sharpshooter, however, the leafhopper experts are silent, although one tropical species, a leafhopper much larger than the blue-green sharpshooter, appears to have evolved a color pattern that makes it look very much like a stinging wasp (complete with yellow banded abdomen and translucent wing covers), a widespread phenomenon among insects as we have seen and will comment on again in the pages ahead. Most persons, however, that study leafhoppers appear interested primarily in the economic impact of certain species, which feed on a wide variety of valuable plants, including of course grapevines. In Europe, grape producers have their own pestilential leafhopper to deal with, one that transmits an equally nasty disease (flavescence dorée) to grapevines. The fascination of many leafhopper workers with vineyards, however, does not mean that leafhopper behavior is irrelevant to their concerns.

Knowing that sexually eager leafhopper males and females communicate with one another by vibrations transmitted through leaves has stimulated research into whether disruption of this premating interaction would help vineyard owners combat the bug (and leafhoppers are true bugs, members of the order Hemiptera, Heteroptera, or Homoptera, depending on your preference). This work is analogous to that with agriculturally destructive moths, which use chemical signals to communicate between the sexes, a finding that has led to the development of a flourishing synthetic sex pheromone industry. Spreading scents that confuse male moths in their search for pheromone-releasing females has in some cases lowered the financial and environmental costs of the pesticide applications that are the traditional method of coping with insect pests. Could synthetic vibrational signals do the same for agriculturalists who must deal with sharpshooters?

Leafhoppers have special abdominal organs that produce sound vibrations that travel from the bug to a leaf and can then be detected a short distance away by another leafhopper either via the antennae (which can pick up the airborne component of the signal) or via the legs (which have receptors that sense substrate-borne vibrations). In some species, males produce a long and complex signal to which receptive females respond with a specific signal of their own that overlaps that of the male, with the bugs singing a duet, if you will. Each species has its own pattern of calling and answering.

A group of European researchers asked whether the production of a loud mimetic vibrational signal could do unto leafhoppers what synthetic pheromones have done unto gypsy moths and cotton bollworm moths. This team used special laser equipment to record the extremely faint messages produced by males of a leafhopper that French winemakers despise and then attached playback devices to the leaves of grapevines. The trick worked. The pseudosignals reduced the mating rate of female leafhoppers by 90 percent or more. Perhaps someday grape producers will regularly employ this novel (and still expensive) method of control of the leafhoppers that do so much damage to their livelihoods.

In the meantime, researchers studying the European leafhopper that is anathema to vineyard owners have found that a tangle-web spider has the ability to eavesdrop on calling individuals. The predator uses the information it overhears to track down and kill the caller, which results in greater mortality for the "noisier" males than for the quieter females, which signal less often than their would-be partners.

Eavesdropping in this system is not confined to predatory spiders inasmuch as males of some leafhoppers listen in on duetting pairs and may either try to mask a rival male's signal with vibrations of their own or hurry over silently to intercept the female before she reaches the calling rival. Not that leafhoppers are unique in the ability of males to interfere with one another by tuning in to the messages that a signaler intends for a particular female. For example, in some katydids, males that hear another male calling approach the caller in an attempt to get to an approaching female first, thereby enjoying the fruits of his labor (without the cost of exposing themselves to eavesdropping predatory bats and the like).

Despite the relative abundance of research on the use of vibrational signals by duetting leafhoppers, I would still like to know if the blue-green sharpshooter's magnificent color pattern has any role to play in the mating system of this insect, which may be insignificant in size but has evolved a thoroughly sophisticated behavioral repertoire.

The Coyote Chorus

February 2013

Winter continues along Deer Creek with temperatures in the thirties when I start my walk this morning. I keep transferring my walking stick from one hand to the other in an attempt to avoid what feels like incipient frostbite of whichever hand is exposed to the cold. But it is sunny and as the morning progresses, my hands, my backpack, and I warm up. Moving west, I find the creek flowing steadily (figure 46). Along the way, a rock squirrel interrupts its morning sunbath on a streamside rock and dashes out of sight into the cover provided by a stony wall carved by past floods.

The sparrows in the area are still congregated in large winter flocks; white-crowned and black-throated sparrows dominate the lower groups (along with some Brewer's sparrows), while farther up the canyon, I encounter one flock composed entirely of dozens of juncos. Overwintering ruby-crowned kinglets hover by the outer branches of the willows, plucking insects and insect eggs from the green catkins and incipient leaves of the plants.

On the hillside to the south, a coyote concert begins and ends in about a minute. Although the singers seem to be fairly close, they are invisible in the dense chaparral in which they are ensconced. As is customary for this species, which has a large vocal repertoire, the sounds they produce

Figure 46. Water is flowing in the creek near the trailhead after sufficient winter precipitation.

vary greatly but on this occasion are primarily composed of a series of yips and yelps, some of which are so high pitched as to resemble whistles. When researchers play tapes of coyote group-yip howls in areas known to be occupied by coyotes, they often get vocalizations from the resident coyotes but much less often from nonresidents. This result suggests that territorial animals use their vocal signals to help them maintain their real estate, perhaps by warning newcomers to get lost before the resident group tracks them down and attacks the intruders.

The relative abundance of water in the stream surely relates to the several storms that have passed through central Arizona in the past month. Just a week ago, it snowed in Tempe, a most unusual event that made the local evening news. But the snow melted almost as soon as it landed in most parts of town. No doubt the snow lasted longer in the Mazatzals, but today just a light smattering of white decorates the red rock ridges high above the creek. Occasionally, I encounter a narrow strip of frozen snow in the permanent shade cast by walls of vegetation

Figure 47. A tributary of Deer Creek that will dry up completely in the weeks ahead.

bordering the trail. But for the most part, the snow has turned to water, much of which has made its way downhill into the stream. When the water tumbles over a rock ledge into a little pool below, a band of transparent bubbles forms on the surface, a signal of the current transitory exuberance of Deer Creek (figure 47).

The storms have greened up the vegetation all along the stream, but flowering is still some time away for most of the plants in the canyon. The exceptions include the willows with their green catkins, the manzanita with their clusters of small white flowers touched with pink, and the silk tassel bushes that have now produced full-sized tassels of pale green that dangle from their branch tips. The shrubs that I inspect closely are primarily male plants, the tassels of which are composed of complex flowers lined up one after the other; the pollen-bearing stamens peek out between paler, almost transparent bands of tissue that enclose the male reproductive organs.

As I move higher and higher into the canyon, the stream gains a little in strength due to the cumulative effect of seeps and streamlets that add their inputs to the creek. After three hours of walking, I stop and rest a little on a rock bench in the middle of the stream before carefully picking my way over to a side canyon. A thin and tattered blanket of snow lines the lower part of the western wall of the canyon where shade reigns most of the day. Just a short distance beyond, a narrow band of water slides down a thirty-foot-high cliff and slips into a shallow circular pool perhaps ten feet in diameter before continuing on to Deer Creek, taking snowmelt on its journey eastward, past the leafless willows and the dead sycamore trunks, still standing after all these years since the fire that swept the canyon clean.

Another Spring

March 2013

The walk today takes place in a landscape that is on the verge of spring. Any number of perennial plants are in flower, including barberry with its small yellow blossoms, willows with their odd greenish inflorescences, and the white-flowered pointleaf manzanita (figure 48a). Of special note are the abundant blue dicks (figure 48b) whose thin leaves surround flower stalks topped with a cluster of blue to magenta to pale pink flowers. The plants have poked up through the dried sprangletop grasses, on hillsides by rocks, everywhere in fact.

Spring annuals too have begun to reproduce, although more individuals and species will be flowering soon. Still, I appreciate the occasional deep orange wallflower by the stream, which is flowing energetically. In addition, for my viewing pleasure, there are several species of lupines that range from tiny to modest in size, the white anemones, two species of lotus peas, one with large flowers and a shrub-like form, the other a little ground cover with minute flowers, and an attractive purplish-flowered plant, a member of the genus *Astragalus*, which contains well over 300 species in the United States. The abundance of species in the genus makes the plants a challenging group for taxonomists, of which I am not one. Suffice it to say that the common name of the group is locoweed in recognition of their ability to poison livestock in ways

Figure 48a. Manzanita's small white flowers signal that spring is here. The circular slits cut in the flowers have been made by nectar thieves, such as carpenter bees, which short-circuit the pollination strategy of the flowers by securing the nectar reward without coming in contact with the pollen-bearing anthers. Photograph by Elizabeth Makings.

Figure 48b. The leaves of Papago onion have now collected sufficient energy from the sun to help the plant produce its small but beautiful purplish flowers.

Figure 48c. One of the many Arizonan locoweeds that is in flower on this spring day.

that cause them to act crazy (and sometimes die). The locoweed that I encounter along Deer Creek Trail is too small and scarce to do much damage to the cattle that occasionally graze here, but I admire the plant for its lovely flowers and for its contribution to the biodiversity of the area (figure 48c).

The warm weather has brought out the harvester ants, which are running around on the barren aprons of soil and pebbles that surround their nest entrances. This time of year they are not aggressive in defense of a brood of winged reproductives because these adults have yet to be produced. Nevertheless, I try not to stand inadvertently next to a nest for any period of time. Once stung by a harvester ant, one develops a strong aversion to a repeat experience with this small but well-protected insect.

Perhaps the strongest signs of spring are the butterflies, of which there are many out and about on this warm day: drab brown-black skippers like the northern dusky wing; mourning cloaks, the dark colors of which are enlivened by a border of yellow along the wing edges; spring azures darting about while adding a dash of blue to the proceedings; and the checkerspots, splashes of orange and black that occupy perches on the trail from which they launch leisurely patrol flights in either direction from their resting spots. The flowering flora and active fauna of the area make it easy to ignore the burnt junipers, which are now about all that remains to remind us of the old fire that came roaring down the creek long ago.

Back to Deer Creek

October 2013

I travel to the Deer Creek area after an absence of over six months spent outside Arizona. My companions are a botanist colleague and my wife, Sue, who long ago renounced her fire-induced dislike of this trail. Near the start of the walk, we spot a sage thrasher, a bird that is either on its way farther south from sage flats in the north or else a bird that may winter near Deer Creek to feed upon the juniper berries from the smattering of junipers that survived the fire. The thrasher is not at all common here in either the fall or the spring, and so it is a treat to see one this morning, flying from mesquite to mesquite, showing off the white tail spots that are one of its diagnostic features.

Shortly thereafter, we begin to flush bands of meadowlarks, which glide away from us in groups of up to a dozen or more. As they cruise off, the birds display their handsome white outer tail feathers. A few land in the burnt but still standing junipers in among the prickly shrubs surrounding them. In this position, they show off their yellow fronts marked at this time of year with smudgy black *V*s.

Note that both the sage thrasher and the meadowlarks possess conspicuous white tail spots or white edges to their tails, a common characteristic of many other species as well. Several behavioral ecologists have thought about this trait and in so doing have produced a number of adaptive explanations for tails of this sort, while acknowledging that the issue is currently unresolved for most species. (However, for a group of warblers that spread and fan their black and white tails, the evidence strongly indicates that they gain foraging benefits by inducing otherwise hidden insects to fly, which makes it easier for the birds to launch successful attacks on their prey.)

One possibility for some species is that the white feathers or patches help individuals keep in touch with others as they fly off, so that individuals are not left behind in places where they might be vulnerable to predatory attack. The flock cohesion hypothesis could apply to meadowlarks in fall or winter, when they occasionally form flocks as we observed, but not sage thrashers, which are generally asocial (although conceivably the tail spots could come into play in helping the male and female members of a pair keep in touch with each other).

Another possibility is that the display of conspicuous feathers by flying birds alerts predators that a potential victim has taken flight and so is unlikely to be easily caught, just as white-tailed deer use their white tail to communicate with those hunting them; if so, it is in the interest of the predator to abandon an attack—a decision that benefits the prey as well.

Yet another hypothesis that has received some support is that the extent of white in tail feathers that are otherwise largely dark reveals something important and useful about the individual to others of the opposite sex. In other words, this feature of bird plumage might play a role in mate choice. Indeed, in the dark-eyed junco, females seem to prefer males with relatively large amounts of white in the tail.

Given the abundance of possible explanations for white-bordered tails in birds, it may not be surprising that more research is needed for particular species before we can claim to have the answer in hand for that animal. I would like more information on why meadowlarks display their white tail feathers in flight as they sail over a scrubby habitat that features dried grasses and large stands of the catclaw mimosa and the equally thorny catclaw acacia. All these years, I have failed to realize that the flats near the lower creek are home to two similar-looking (but very different) spiny species, one a mimosa and the other an acacia. My

Figure 49. A stunning wasp-mimicking moth inspecting the leaves of a local primrose on the only day on which I have seen this species. Photograph by Elizabeth Makings.

botanical knowledge still leaves a lot to be desired, as does my understanding of bird plumage.

Leaving the meadowlarks to their own diversions, we find a surprising number of plants in flower in the waterless creek, plants that are attracting carpenter bees and syrphid flies, as well as an assortment of butterflies. While in the band of sand and cobbles bordering the creek bed, I see a wasp flying slowly close to the ground in among the grasses—except it is not a wasp but a moth with yellow- and black-banded abdomen, orange antennae, and small wings with deep orange patches. A marvelous wasp mimic. We follow it around hoping for a photograph, but it keeps flying until it finds a clump of leaves of a stemless primrose that has white flowers when in bloom but only leaves at this time of year. The moth-wasp lands and wanders about the leaves (figure 49), occasionally appearing to oviposit, although we never actually see an egg emerge from its abdomen. A moth enthusiast tells us later that we have seen a member of the species *Euhagena nebraskae*, a moth not previously known to occur in Arizona. But when I look for images of this species, I come across an Internet site where I can compare *E. nebraskae* with several other members of the genus. To my admittedly untrained eye, we have seen a female of the guara borer moth, *E. emphytiformis*, not *E. nebraskae*. If so, we have encountered a moth that is already known from a few locales in Arizona. The species is, however, a rare one, as befits a wasp mimic that gains a protective advantage only if the models (true stinging wasps) greatly outnumber the edible mimics (assuming that the moth is edible). Certainly, if I were an insectivorous bird and I saw the moth looking and behaving like a paper wasp, of which there are many along Deer Creek, I would leave the mimic very much alone.

Upstream, the sycamores and willows are increasingly abundant and much taller and denser than they were even a year ago, especially in the portions of the stream where water has oozed its way to the surface. At the stretch of the stream where bare red rock slides down to a pool with a stand of cattails, a favorite destination of mine in recent years, we find a large skipper that appears to be probing damp spots on the water-smoothed rocks with its curved proboscis. Males of the Arizona giant skipper (*Agathymus aryxna*) are said to drink from such spots, whereas females neither feed nor drink during their short adult lives. The skipper is a drab grey creature but a big one, with a much fatter, stubbier abdomen than a "typical" skipper.

The big spreadwing damselfly is present in the willows that border the rocks where the skippers congregate. There are not as many as were present in October 2010, but they are still abundant enough for us to observe the egg-laying behavior of the damselfly. A female in tandem with her partner inserts her eggs into a willow branchlet above the trickle of water that is flowing down to the cattail pool. Scanning the willows for pairs, we find one in which a male holds a female with a rigid abdomen that is not bent into the upside-down U that precedes egg laying. At the end of the long, straight abdomen, a black jumping spider with a red top to its abdomen has inserted its formidable mandibles in the insect. The pierced female is utterly dead but her partner refuses to release her (figure 50).

Figure 50. A large jumping spider has pierced a female spreadwing damselfly with its jaws, killing her prior to feeding upon her body. The male apparently remains oblivious to his ex-partner's demise.

Three years ago, I had observed this same species of spider (*Phiddipus johnsoni*) feeding on a female, although no male was attached to the damselfly at that time. The dead female subsequently attracted a single male then, despite the fact that his "mate" was in no condition to do anything, let alone accept sperm from a sexually eager male. The necrophilic behavior of the male damselfly speaks volumes about the low threshold for sexual activity in males of this (and many other) species.

While I was photographing the ménage à trois, the spider suddenly released its meal and leapt to another branch. There it confronted another spider of the same species. The two spiders grappled vigorously, and, in short order, the damselfly killer dispatched the intruder as well. The attacker then apparently fed upon the other spider, the body of which shrank over time, presumably because the contents of the loser were siphoned off into the larger winner.

As noted before, cannibalism is not uncommon among spiders, a group in which smaller males are at risk of winding up in the jaws of would-be mates (see page 85). But here, a male has killed and eaten another male, an action that has several potential benefits for the successful cannibal. First, the bigger male has removed a competitor for the damselflies and other insects that constitute its prey in the streamside band of willows. Second, the cannibal has acquired another meal composed of biochemicals that are very likely to be useful because the victim and the cannibal are made up of the same materials, which might facilitate the recycling of these substances from the victim to the consumer. Gary Meffe and Marty Crump showed that mosquito fish that consumed processed food composed of other mosquito fish appeared to grow heavier and reproduce sooner than those fed similar sorts of food made up of other fish or other edible items.

The nutritional bonus hypothesis for cannibalism may apply to mosquito fish but not necessarily to other species, such as spiders the females of which dispatch males from time to time. In one study of an occasionally cannibalistic spider, females that were given a choice clearly preferred to eat crickets rather than males of their own species, a result suggesting that members of the same species are *not* necessarily nutritionally superior to other kinds of edible items. But the fact that the jumping spider left a presumably perfectly edible damselfly to assault a male of his own species, surely a dangerous move, suggests that cannibalistic jumping spiders gain from the decision to tackle a fellow male. Any nutritional benefits they derive may be a bonus that comes from dispatching a rival for food or mates or both.

Meadowlarks and sage thrashers do not belong to the fraternity of cannibalistic species. Yes, individuals of both species compete vigorously with one another for space and mates during the breeding season, but then meadowlarks, at least, may pacifically seek out the company of their fellows once the competitive phase of the year is over. By being social, they probably secure a certain amount of protection thanks to the improved vigilance provided by others in the group or, alternatively, to the distractions that their companions offer should a Cooper's hawk come hunting for them in an open field. Not so for males of the black and red jumping spider, an apparently relentless individualistic predator capable of killing damselflies much larger than itself or rivals of its own species. As an admirer of all creatures great and small, I like seeing both bloodthirsty spiders and sociable meadowlarks here on the edge of Deer Creek on a fall day in 2013.

Winter, Arizona Style

December 2013

In many parts of the country, the temperatures at 8:30 on a December morning would be frigid, in the single digits, maybe even below zero in the northern tier of states, but here it is merely cool, with temperatures in the forties, with the day quickly warming up to the low sixties. The sun is out, as it usually is, although some high, thin clouds foster a weak impression of a winter's day.

Meadowlarks are still around in good numbers; I see them cruising over the flats with their white tail feathers in view. They are joined by multiple flocks of white-crowned sparrows, as well as a few western bluebirds that often spend the winter here near the creek. Year-round resident birds include the canyon towhee, the spotted towhee, the western scrub jay, and the black-throated sparrow. Considerably farther up the creek, at somewhat higher elevations, I run into a flock of juncos, then a gaggle of bushtits, some ruby-crowned kinglets, and one bridled titmouse, all taking advantage of the willows the yellowed leaves of which probably provide habitat for overwintering insects and insect eggs. Of course, no spreadwing damselflies or jumping spiders are out and about today.

The stream is flowing through the creek bed to a point about a half mile west of the junction with the main branch of Deer Creek. The

Figure 51a. The willows with their feet in the water of the stream have grown substantially since the Willow Fire swept down the canyon in 2004. They are now dormant, waiting for the warmer days with longer photoperiods that will be here soon enough.

water supports not just the band of willows but young and resprouted sycamores, a handful of baby cottonwoods, odds and ends of salt cedar, and some mulleins in the loose rocks and sand near the stream (figures 51a and 51b). The salt cedar and mulleins are nonnative intruders, but they add to the biodiversity of the place. Admittedly, exotic species have largely earned very bad press over the years, as they often transform environments and push out the native plant species that once occupied an area. The issue of exotics and their ecological effects has become so widely recognized that there now is an entire journal devoted to the subject, *Biological Invasions*, first published in 1999.

Neither salt cedar nor mullein is common along Deer Creek—yet. Moreover, there is considerable evidence that salt cedar is far less damaging than one would imagine given its reputation as a water guzzling, competitive terror that destroys stream bank habitats once it gains a foothold there. Juliet Stromberg and her colleagues argue that salt

Figure 51b. A young sycamore has a long ways to go before it joins the older, taller specimens already growing in the riparian zone of Deer Creek.

cedar uses no more water than other native riparian species and that eradication of the plant has not led to increased water flows in western rivers. In addition, the spread of salt cedar along many waterways has taken place after a variety of human-caused disturbances, not prior to these influences, and therefore the plant may well have not been directly responsible for declines in native species like cottonwoods and willows. The tamarisk case shows how easy it is for people to demonize introduced species as alien invasives without careful analysis of the evidence.

Be that as it may, I am not saddened by the current scarcity of salt cedar in Deer Creek. In a way, it is surprising that the plant has managed to invade the narrow riparian zone given that it had to have come in after the Willow Fire, within the last decade, almost certainly traveling a long distance to establish a beachhead of sorts in the gravel and loose rocks of the stream bed.

The very few plants flowering here today are hardly overburdened with blooms or fruit. The local sweetbush in the jumbled rocks far down the creek do still have a handful of flowers that are continuing to attract some butterflies, a fritillary here, a little blue there, a couple of checkered skippers, and a sulphur of some sort. The land beside the stream supports some insects besides butterflies, although the grasshopper populations that were so large in the early months of fall have dwindled greatly. I do disturb a few Wheeler's blue-winged grasshoppers as I hike up the narrow trail that winds into the canyon to the west. They flutter off, blue wings on display, until they drop into the grasses nearby. I presume that the larger ones are females and the much smaller ones are males. The pattern of large females and small males is standard for a great many insects, including the vast majority of grasshoppers. It is common in many parts of the world to see a little male hopper riding a big female like a jockey on a horse except that, unlike a jockey, the male grasshopper is copulating with his mount.

The widespread occurrence of sexual size dimorphisms with large females and smaller, often much smaller, males has piqued the interest of biologists perhaps in part because the human species is one in which the sexual size dimorphism is reversed, with men about 10 percent taller than women. Among the insects, the hypothesis for the standard relationship focuses on the benefits of body size for female fecundity. The larger the female, the more eggs she can produce in her lifetime and, thus, the more offspring she can have. Large body size has no comparable advantages for males of many insects, especially in those species in which males simply try to outrace competitors to receptive females.

Winners have plenty of sperm, which are much smaller than eggs, with which to fertilize all the eggs of their partner(s).

In contrast, there are insects in which males fight for access to mates. In species of this sort, large body size should help males pound their rivals into submission, and so we would expect that in these aggressive species, males should approximate females in weight or even exceed the mass of their sexual partners, eliminating or reversing the typical sexual size dimorphism of insects in general. This prediction has been checked many times in insects (and other animals) with gratifying results for persons who find evolutionary theory useful for understanding patterns in nature. In the bee *Centris pallida*, a favorite of mine that occurs at lower elevations than those at Deer Creek, males often do wrestle with opponents in order to acquire a receptive female emerging from an underground brood cell where she spent much of the preceding year. In this species, some males are, as predicted, larger than the largest females. Moreover, big males do win battles for mates and so wind up making a larger proportion of the mating class of males. Being a big bruiser is indeed helpful for a male's reproductive success in this highly physical species (and many others with similar mating systems).

The fact that in our own species males are somewhat larger on average than females suggests that physical aggression among males has played a role in our evolution, albeit not nearly as strongly as in the evolution of our close relatives, the common chimpanzee and the gorilla, both species known for their strongly reversed sexual size dimorphism. Perhaps women are also the product of selection for relatively large bodies, which can come in handy when carting large infants around, something our female ancestors almost certainly had to do while foraging for food in the wild. If true, the size difference between men and women would be reduced in our species—and it is.

Speculations of this sort keep me entertained during the return phase of my hike along Deer Creek, a walk during which I encounter neither man nor woman on this pleasant winter's day.

Robins in Winter

February 2014

On this the first day of February, the mood is far more wintery along Deer Creek than it was on the December day in 2013 when I was last here. Although the billowing clouds above the Mazatzals seem at first to be about to break up, instead they thicken and go on to provide a day of nearly complete overcast. I wear my jacket for almost the entire time I am hiking up and back along the south fork of the stream. In fact, for a few moments, a light mix of rain and slushy snowflakes falls on those of us who are wandering along the stream or hunting for quail on the flat fields to the east of the mountains. The momentary precipitation is merely a reminder of how dry it has been here for more than the past month. Almost no plants are in flower, and instead, the little lupines and other annuals are either totally absent or on hold at an inch or so in height.

But here and there, flocks of robins leave their perches in the dead junipers and fly off toward the south. Over the course of the morning and early afternoon, many groups of up to a dozen or more birds pound off, outlined against the grey skies, providing movement in an otherwise nearly motionless environment. The bands of robins come up steadily from the stream bed where the birds have been drinking and bathing in isolated pools that are ringed with willows, leafless in their winter outfits. Who knows what they expect to find farther south, but eventually they will have to turn around to migrate north to their summer breeding grounds. A few of these handsome birds perch long enough before resuming their journey to let us see their red-orange bellies, grey backs, black heads, and white eye-rings.

The only other winter visitors to the Mazatzals that are abundant today are white-crowned sparrows, great flocks of which react to our approach by scattering into the thickets of mimosa and acacia where they forage and await the arrival of spring. The clouds press down on the land. A profound silence rules except for the low chuckling of the stream in places where the water still flows to the east.

In the early afternoon, the clouds part long enough to let the sun shine on the edge of the stream. Two mourning cloak butterflies suddenly appear and fly along the rocks and dried weeds, perching briefly first in one spot then another. Then the clouds push together again and the temperature, which had risen noticeably during the short sunny spell, plummets. In the chilly air, one of the butterflies cruises east for a bit before turning back to head upstream. It settles on a bank of loose rocks and exposed rootlets. The wings of the mourning cloak open and close, open and close, as the insect creeps into a tiny cave with a roof of slate. Inside the crevice, the only visible sign of the butterfly is the slightly crinkled outer edge of its two wings, pressed together (figure 52). To all intents and purposes, the immobile creature has disappeared, hidden from view in conditions that would have made flight difficult or impossible for any butterfly, cold-blooded as they are.

Mourning cloaks are one of those lepidopterans that apparently overwinter as adults in temperate climes, a minority of all butterfly species but an interesting minority to be sure. These butterflies are long-lived; many of those flying early in the year are noticeably tattered and worn thanks to a long and active life interrupted by spells of hiding in the nooks and crannies that they utilize during cold periods (and during hot summer months as well). Judging from the mourning cloak the behavior of which revealed its hiding place, it would be very hard to find an individual that has slipped unobserved inside a crevice of some sort or under a patch of loose bark.

Figure 52. The yellow wing edge of a mourning cloak butterfly that has crawled into a crevice to hide during a spell when overcast skies and cool temperatures make flight difficult for a butterfly. Photograph by Elizabeth Makings.

Warm weather in early spring provides the cues that trigger activity on the part of overwintering mourning cloaks, which are often the first butterflies seen round and about in cold temperate habitats. Climate change may well induce adult mourning cloaks and others like them to become active sooner than they did in the past. According to Sarah Diamond and her colleagues, overwintering adults, pupae, and caterpillars of a variety of butterflies are indeed appearing earlier and earlier in the year in the United Kingdom, presumably in response to a gradually warming European climate.

I, a warm-blooded animal, although incapable of flight on my own dime at any time, continue to walk slowly downstream on my two hind legs under wintery skies. I am glad to have remembered to bring a jacket with me today.

Yet Another Spring

March 2014

Southern Arizona has been under the influence of a prolonged spell of well-above-average temperatures. While the rest of the nation, or at least the eastern half, has been dealing with repeated incursions of the polar vortex and one snowstorm after another, the highs here have been in the upper seventies or eighties for so long that an early morning reading in the fifties feels downright frigid. Today is no exception to the rule; no jacket or sweater is needed when I get out of the car at the Deer Creek trailhead.

The warm weather has encouraged the overwintering birds to move out, with the result that there are no flocks of meadowlarks, robins, or sparrows here today. On the other hand, the local plants have grown vigorously under the mild weather conditions with the result that a fine diversity of flowering species is on display for this time of year. Some twining mariposa lilies sport their almost absurdly attractive white blossoms in the flats to the east of the canyon, although many more are to come, judging from the specimens still in bud along the trail. The pasture is also home to large patches of a low ground cover composed of tiny lupines, almost all of which are blooming simultaneously. Farther along the trail, at least three other more robust species of lupines are in flower, advertising the great diversity in this huge genus. The glorious white flowers of a stemless primrose have begun to crumple and turn pinkish, their twenty-four hours of life nearly over. I have not spoken of the yellow desert marigolds, the deep pink Arizona penstemons, the scarlet Indian paintbrushes, the pale pink globes of Pringle manzanita (the pointleaf manzanita has already produced its green fruits, some of which are turning dark red). A Goodding's verbena with blue-purple inflorescences has attracted a couple of big bumblebee hawkmoths (probably *Hemaris thetis*) that probe each flower in turn. Owl's clover, always a favorite of mine, stands low but erect in among the grasses, showing off its reddish-purple bracts. Indeed, we are offered a botanical smorgasbord today, complete with a full spectrum of butterflies as well, mourning cloaks, checkerspots, dusky wing skippers, two-tailed swallowtails, and more for the entertainment of the entomologically inclined.

Speaking of insects, the harvester ants are active today, running into and out of their nest entrances as if in a hurry to get somewhere and then right back. Their nests are very conspicuous because the workers actively remove all vegetation from the ground above their underground burrows, creating a circle of barren soil of variable size. The ants in the nest in front of me now have destroyed all the vegetation in a nest circle at least two meters in diameter. Hypotheses abound for the ants' willingness to spend their time and energy making the disk around the nest entrance vegetation-free. Do they do so to help foragers hurry back unimpeded over the last few meters of their trips carrying seeds or other foods they have collected? Do they make this investment in order to expose predators, such as horned lizards, to enemies of their own, the better to discourage a predator from settling in to feast on ants where they are most numerous? Or do they remove the plants above their nest to enable the ground to warm up more quickly, which in turn helps the workers set out early in the morning on their foraging trips?

A number of researchers have explored one or another of these hypotheses. For example, Ave Marie Bucy and Michael Breed erected shades over nest mounds and found that the ants in the nests below were slower to begin foraging than those with unshaded nest disks. On the other hand, the ants in the experimentally covered nests were able to

Figure 53. The barren circular disk of soil above a *Pogonomyrmex* harvester ant nest is surrounded by a ring of goldfield daisies in flower.

keep foraging longer than workers in the colonies that were not shaded. Presumably it is usually more productive for ants to be on the search for food early in the day before seed patches and the like have been depleted by workers from neighboring colonies than to be able to keep foraging later on.

The nest is made all the more conspicuous by a surrounding rim of bright yellow–flowered goldfield daisies, each plant only a few inches high but collectively forming a bright yellow circle around the brown nest apron (figure 53). It seems likely that these plants grew from seeds discarded by the ants outside the barren disk area. Harvester ants do sometimes throw away seeds that they have brought into the nest either by mistake or because they are able to replace seeds of lesser value with those that are more nutritious as the harvesting season proceeds. By tossing out unwanted materials from the nest, the ants enrich the soil around the disk, creating conditions that enable surviving seeds to grow robustly, as appears to be the case for the encircling ring of flowering goldfields.

Figure 54. A clump of the little barley (*Hordeum pusillum*), a native species that has colonized the ground adjacent to Deer Creek.

Another plant of note seen along Deer Creek today is the little barley (figure 54), a species much smaller and only distantly related to its congener, the European or domesticated barley, the grass that the U.S. Forest Service traditionally employed to reduce erosion in the first year after a major wildfire (see page 17). *Wikipedia* tells me that the little barley (and it is barely six inches high, if that) has evolved from related species in southern South America before somehow skipping over the tropics and arriving in North America. I wonder how the little grass managed to negotiate its long journey north.

Wikipedia also informs me that the seeds of little barley are edible. Evidence exists that some Amerindians cultivated the grass several thousand years ago as a food source before switching to more productive agricultural crops, such as corn. I am not about to try to harvest the little barley but am simply happy to know that a nonintroduced barley is living here as part of the natural complex of grasses and other plants that live in this delightful part of the world.

Plant Colors and
Plant Visitors

April 2014

Before heading off for another prolonged stay on the family farm in northern Virginia, I decide to squeeze in one more visit to Deer Creek, particularly since I had heard through the grapevine that the mariposa lilies were going gangbusters in the flats leading up to the creek. The grapevine was right. Instead of scattered lilies poking up near a prickly pear cactus or through one or another spiny shrub, the plants were flowering here, there, and everywhere. In fact, many flowers had passed their prime and had begun to twist and wither. Some had even produced their thin seed capsules, an indicator of the march of the seasons.

A mariposa lily that has been pollinated but still possesses an old flower is a quite different creature from the open-faced, white-petalled objet d'art that it once was. The undersurface of the petals of a senescent flower, which now has lost its symmetry, are colored pink-magenta. I wonder if the color communicates to would-be insect visitors that the flower has already been pollinated and can be avoided, indeed should be avoided in the interests of maximizing the visitor's efficient collection of resources from unpollinated flowers. Long ago, Karl von Frisch established that honey bees have good color vision and they use it when foraging for nectar and pollen. To the extent that other bees and pollinators have similar abilities, the use of visual signals of this sort could account for the conspicuous (to us) colors of the flowers of many plants, including the stemless primrose that grows along the edge of the creek and up hillsides. The gloriously large, fresh flowers of this species are stark white and presumably easy for hawkmoths and carpenter bees to locate during the single evening when the flowers produce nectar to reward pollinating insects. But within twenty-four hours, flowers that were once vibrant become crinkled and withered, while the color of the primrose changes from stark white to pink (figure 55). I presume that the color change is adaptive for the plant in helping pollinators locate unpollinated flowers rather than wasting their time with senescent pollinated blooms.

If this view is correct, the color of a flower can serve as a signal to insects and others that promotes the well-being of the pollinators as well as the plant by making its old flowers easy to identify. Of course, flower color can also communicate that a flower deserves attention from observant pollinators, as in the bright whites of unpollinated mariposa

Figure 55. The flowers of the stemless primrose change color (and form) dramatically as they age over the course of a day.

lilies and stemless primroses. Along Deer Creek today, a host of plants have produced fresh flowers the conspicuous colors of which, notably red, may announce the availability of nectar and/or pollen to insect harvesters of these resources. Among the red- or reddish-flowered plants are Arizona penstemons, four-o'clocks, fairy dusters, Indian paintbrush, owl's clover, hedgehog cacti, the littleleaf ratany, and more. The penstemons have tubular flowers of the sort most easily probed by long-billed birds, notably hummingbirds. Red is said to be a color that these birds readily detect and quickly associate with food, namely the nectar found deep within the corolla. Anyone who has hiked with a red pack on his or her back knows that hummingbirds are prone to inspect these items, presumably mistaking them for a flower with a food reward to end all rewards.

Although bees are often said to be more attracted to blue flowers than red ones, some plants use red, nontubular flowers to draw in bees, not hummingbirds. Fairy dusters have flat, splayed flowers that bees find perfectly acceptable, and this is even truer of the large, open, reddish-purple flowers of hedgehog cacti, to which relatively large bees come to bumble about among the forest of moving stamens at the base of the flowers. The typical preference of bees for blue flowers is probably a function of the fact that bee color vision is such that red flowers are harder for them to detect against a green background, which means that they can usually collect more nectar per unit time at easier-to-find flowers, such as blue ones. If bees specialize on blue flowers, birds (with their different visual systems) can forage optimally on those that are not blue, such as red flowers.

Red could also be a signal that a fruit is ready to harvest. The reddish-tinged fruits of the manzanita really do look like little apples, as the Spanish name for the plant suggests. Consumers that avoid green fruits in favor of those that have changed color may well derive more calories and nutrients from their selections than those that eat fruits without regard to their color. Perhaps this is why the mature fruits of lotus peas are a dark red as well. Red color is sometimes produced by anthocyanin-rich pigments (see page 133), and anthocyanins are antioxidants. Therefore, if birds were to use anthocyanin reds to distinguish between fruits of rich versus poor quality, they could derive nutritional benefits from their choices.

But the picture is almost certainly more complex than just indicated. First, do flower pollinators or fruit consumers (and thus seed dispersers) see colors in much the same way that we do? If they do not, and as just noted, bees, for example, have more difficulty discriminating red things against a green background than we do, then we could be mistaken in thinking that a particular color is responsible for the attraction of a consumer when instead it might be something else, like the degree of contrast, as perceived by the signal receiver, between the flower or fruit and the background on which it occurs.

Moreover, some red plant parts may not have evolved to communicate with visiting consumers of various sorts. Take the red-brown limbs of manzanita, or the reddish tops of red brome, an especially abundant nonnative grass growing along Deer Creek. These colors might be simply the nonadaptive side effects of the biochemical processes underlying the production of bark and seed heads. On the other hand, they could be signals to potential herbivores that the plant is either difficult to eat or well protected chemically.

One also wonders about the young stems of the fragrant sumac, which are red-purple instead of green (figure 56a). Ditto for the young leaves of the scrubby oaks growing by the stream, which are a deep red-brown instead of the traditional green of mature oak leaves (figure 56b). Work in the tropics, where red younger leaves are common in tropical trees, suggests that the color red signals low levels of nitrogen in the leaves, which reduces their nutritive value to herbivores. As a result, leaf eaters may favor older, greener leaves instead, although these items may be tougher or better protected chemically in other ways. At least in tropical ecosystems, red-leafed seedlings do survive better than members of other species whose leaves more quickly turn green. The survival advantage of red-leafed species comes, however, at the cost of a reduction in growth, a finding consistent with the hypothesis that red leaves lack the photosynthetic abilities of green ones.

Yet, as is so often the case, the picture is cloudy with respect to the adaptive value of red young leaves that take time to turn green, just

Figure 56a. The young stems of the fragrant sumac are red-purple, unlike the older, greener stems (see also figure 41).

Figure 56b. The young leaves of the shrub live oaks are often an intense red-brown, whereas the older, mature leaves are green.

as uncertainty still rules in the analysis of the adaptive value, if any, of mature red and yellow autumn leaves. As it turns out, in the young leaves of tropical trees, anthocyanins are often involved in producing the color red. If these are antioxidant pigments like those that turn fruits red, one might think that herbivores would actively seek out young reddish leaves and thereby acquire a health-promoting food—but they apparently do not. However, as just noted above, many insects and most mammals have visual systems very different from ours, so that they may not even see the color red. Indeed, red leaves probably appear dark to many herbivores, which raises questions about the signal value of the appearance of these leaves. Perhaps red leaves simply appear dead to many insects and plant-eating mammals, which could account for the willingness of these herbivores to overlook young leaves that postpone turning green.

In other words, the significance, if any, of young red leaves needs further examination, not the most satisfactory of conclusions but an honest one, perhaps, that reflects the complexity of communication by color signals in the plant and animal world.

Back to Deer Creek Again

October 2014

After having been away in northern Virginia for about six months, I am back at Deer Creek for a tenth-year reunion after the fire. Thanks to a strong monsoon, which deposited record amounts of rain in greater Phoenix about a month ago, the upper part of the south fork of Deer Creek has some flowing water, and the surrounding country-side is positively lush with patches of delicate green grasses a good eighteen inches tall waving in the light breezes on this very warm October morning. Even the fields of sprangletop grasses, now a dried-out golden tan rather than a lively green, have the look of a dense prairie in fall, a prairie dotted with stands of prickly pear cacti, some with dark red fruits still waiting for a glyptodont to come along.

I see many familiar plants, some patches of the longleaf false gold-eneye flowering enthusiastically on the southern side of the creek, tall willows with leaves turning yellow in the creek proper, sycamores ever more treelike, and an assortment of purple tansyasters, many having set seed while a minority remain in flower. Broom snakeweed, another aster but a yellow shrub not a small, purple-flowered plant, is blooming profusely in the lower pastures on the way to the creek itself. A red star morning glory flaunts its bright red tubular flowers (see figure 38) as if to say that it is not at all concerned about having been named a noxious plant species in Arizona. This plant, like most of the common smaller species along Deer Creek, possesses toxins and repellents that make it unattractive to cattle, which is why it not only has survived here but has flourished in what has been for many years a cow-dominated habitat.

No doubt as a result of the abundance of grasses and other plants, grasshoppers abound, especially the red-winged grasshopper, which pops up along the trail to flutter off noisily to a new hiding place after briefly displaying its deep red hind wings in flight.

But I do encounter some insects that I have either rarely or never seen in this part of Arizona before. A northern white-skipper perches obligingly on a stalk of a buckwheat; the tiny checkerspot, a very small butterfly indeed, flies slowly to a twig, where it sits while sedately opening and shutting its wings; a monarch butterfly cruises purposefully down the creek bed toward me before swerving away. I assume that the monarch is migrating to a winter home somewhere along the Pacific coast or perhaps to a mountain retreat in Mexico. I later confirm my guess by checking the Internet site of Southwest Monarch Study, a group that captures, tags, and releases monarchs in the Southwest during the fall months. Recaptures of butterflies tagged in Arizona have been made both on the Californian coast and in the mountains near Mexico City.

Monarch butterflies in the eastern United States are much better known than their western cousins for their extraordinary migration, which begins each spring, when monarchs from overwintering sites high in the Mexican mountains travel north to the southern United States. There, mated females lay eggs on milkweed plants, creating a second generation that as adults continues to travel north in search of fresh milkweeds. The summer brings a third and fourth generation as well. Some of these butterflies reach the northern United States and southern Canada, starting points for a return migration of up to 2,000 miles to the oyamel firs growing high in the mountains of central Mexico, where the successful migrators will spend the winter dangling from the trees in roosts containing many thousands of semicomatose monarchs. With warming weather, the surviving monarchs set out along a northward route that will bring them, if all goes well, back to the United States and the milkweeds found there.

As noted much earlier, persons monitoring the number of monarchs that reside in the Mexican wintering sites have discovered that the population of monarchs has plummeted in recent decades. Biologists, among them Lincoln Brower, have been attempting to determine the cause for the population collapse of what was once a very common species. Debate continues on the reason(s) why. Among the possible contributing factors are illegal logging in the Mexican forest preserves that overwintering monarchs utilize and the loss of North American milkweeds to herbicides, housing developments, and the like. Much attention has been directed at genetically modified, herbicide-resistant corn and soybeans, which are now widely grown in the midwestern states (the heartland of milkweeds used by monarch caterpillars). Roundup Ready corn, soybeans, and other crops enable farmers to spray Roundup herbicide with abandon on farm fields that once supported not just agriculturally valuable plants but also many milkweeds and other plants. These incidental "crops" no longer exist but were critical for the production of monarch caterpillars (figure 57) as indicated by the tight correlation between the rapid spread of Roundup Ready crops since 1996 and the subsequent sharp decline of eastern monarch populations.

So what can be done to help maintain the wonderful migratory pattern of the eastern monarch butterflies? Brower and the Center for Biological Diversity have petitioned the federal government to declare the monarch butterfly a threatened species. The process of instituting such a declaration is a lengthy one, during which time the monarch may become so scarce that they may cease to migrate in force to Mexico. Moreover, it could well be as some colleagues of Brower have noted, that if the monarch or its migration were federally declared to be endangered, farmers and Monsanto (the producer of Roundup Ready crop seeds) would probably refuse to cooperate with those eager to assist the butterfly. In addition, if the loss of remaining nonagricultural lands continues at its current pace (over two million acres of milkweed habitat converted to condominiums, parking lots, and factories per year in the United States, according to Monarch Watch), the monarch will be in terrible trouble no matter what its federally mandated conservation status. Chip Taylor of Monarch Watch urges us to plant milkweeds in

Figure 57. Two monarch butterfly caterpillars on the primary food plant of eastern monarchs, the common milkweed, in the spring of 2014; the two caterpillars are consuming plants that were moved by the author to a flower border on the family farm in northern Virginia.

our gardens and advises the authorities to let the plant grow to maturity along roadsides instead of mowing the verges so often that that median strips look like lawns. Nonetheless, it is hard to be hopeful about the future of the monarch either in Mexico, where illegal tree cutting continues in monarch preserves, or in the United States, where population growth, economic demand, the loss of milkweed-containing farmland, and the commercial power of Monsanto are on the increase.

For the moment, however, it is appropriate to applaud when one sees a monarch caterpillar on a milkweed or even one adult butterfly on the move to its winter refugium. Applaud, I do.

Crab Spiders

It is a pleasure to wander along the trail to the south fork of Deer Creek on a spring day, even if the temperatures are more than ten degrees above normal. In fact, the new normal is downright hot by the time I return to the car about 1 p.m. But the rain of a little more than a week ago must have reached the Mazatzals because the fields and canyons are green, the flowing water in the creek has reached well down the south fork of the stream, and many of the plants are flowering profusely. The shrubby deer brush in particular is blooming as if there were no tomorrow with masses of tiny white flowers covering each limb and twig. The yellow barberries are all aglow and the mountain mahoganies have put out an unusually great number of their small yellow flowers as well, which nicely complement the little green beech-like leaves of this Deer Creek shrub. And the smaller flowering plants are all in their places along the trail, accenting the walk with their whites, reds, blues, and yellows; the big white-flowered primroses flourishing as always in the spring in the broad flat that surrounds the stream crossing; the red Indian paintbrush poking out of the one hiding place where I have found them in the past; the little blue lupines carpeting the rise above the stream where they are regularly seen in the early springtime; and the desert marigolds scattered here and there on the slopes that contain the running wash. True, the owl's clover has just begun to peek through the dried grasses on the plain that leads to an upper stream crossing, but a few of these small relatives of the Indian paintbrush have joined their fellow plants in producing mature flowers to entertain the photographer in me.

Of all the flowering plants that make my hike enjoyable today, perhaps the most noticeably abundant ones are the blue dicks or wild hyacinths, a lily that occurs almost everywhere as scattered ones or twos in the gravelly flats or in much larger bands on hillsides. Although they are generally less than a foot tall, their small blue to magenta to pink flowers are held conspicuously in small clusters on the top of thin, dark stalks that rise out of the base of the plants. As noted before, the bulbs of this plant are said to be edible, and Amerindians apparently put this claim to the test, which is why the plant is sometimes christened the Papago onion. But its aesthetic side invariably trumps its culinary component as far as I am concerned.

I am not the only creature drawn to these plants. A gorgeous two-tailed swallowtail hangs from the flowers of a blue dick, demonstrating beautifully why it was selected as Arizona's state butterfly. Several other butterfly species visit the blue dicks along the trail during my hike, but this is the only individual of the two-tailed swallowtail that I see foraging at the plant today.

In addition to butterflies, several species of bee flies appear to be interested in the nectar contained within the flowers of this plant, and their visits in turn have attracted the attention of some local crab spiders. These predators have taken up residence in the flowers in order to ambush nectar-searching flies. Over the course of my four-hour hike, I find two bee flies dangling from the jaws of whitish-purple crab spiders ensconced in a terminal cluster of blue dick flowers. Although the biology of blue dicks has not been studied in much detail (I find only two papers on the plant in the Web of Science), crab spiders have been the subject of much research (using "crab spider" as a search phrase revealed dozens of articles in the Web of Science). Some studies were purely taxonomic (with, for example, the author describing a previously undescribed species) but others focused on such things as the avoidance of flowers by bumblebees that had been grasped (but not hurt) mimicking an unsuccessful crab spider attack (as simulated by squeezing the body of a visiting insect).

Spiders vary in the stratagems they use to locate productive wait-and-ambush sites and to prey upon pollinators that visit the flowers that the spiders occupy. So, for example, some spider species match the background provided by their ambush spot, an ability that has long been thought to help camouflage the predator so that edible pollinators will come close enough to be captured by the spider. The color match between some crab spiders and the flowers can be achieved *after* the predators have taken up residence in a particular flower.

However, some more recent research casts grave doubt on the camouflage hypothesis, at least for certain crab spider species, of which there are many, because some of these small predators fail to change color when moving among flowers of different hues. In fact, some crab spiders appear to sit conspicuously on flowers whose color is not at all similar to that of the spider. These predators may be reflecting patches of ultraviolet radiation, a cue that at least some pollinators apparently use to identify flowers of species that usually provide good nectar or pollen rewards. I wonder if the two crab spiders that I find holding bee flies on some blue dicks today belong to a species of deceitful ultraviolet reflectors; the body color of these spiders is white with a dash of pink or purple (figure 58). Another crab spider, possibly of the same species, has, however, adopted a pale blueish color that more or less matches that of the blue dick on which the spider is perched.

At least one study found no support for *either* the camouflage hypothesis *or* the prey attraction hypothesis, leading the authors to conclude that those crab spiders that do match the color of the flowers on which they rest must do so for reasons other than to make themselves harder to detect. Just what these other factors may be remains to be discovered (there is little support for the possibility that crab spiders that color match make it harder for their predators to find them). For the time being, we probably have to content ourselves with acceptance of the point that the validity of hypotheses about crab spider coloration almost certainly depends on the species of spider studied and the kind

Figure 58a. A whitish crab spider that occurs on blue dick flowers, where it ambushes flies (such as the bee fly it has in its jaws) that come to visit the flowers or perhaps are drawn by the color of the spider itself.

Figure 58b. A bright yellow crab spider that occurs on yellow flowers whose color the spider matches—to conceal itself from its predators or its prey, such as the rather ordinary fly that it has killed here? Or for some other reason?

of prey available to it, which might explain why a number of researchers found no positive effect of conspicuousness on prey visitation.

In the meantime, a moribund, furry bee fly dangles from the jaws of a crab spider residing in the flower of a blue dick. Some prey obviously make fatal mistakes when seeking out the flowers of this plant. Although the fly is dead, very dead, the vegetation on the surrounding hillside and creek are mostly alive and green. Indeed, the skinny willows in and along the creek itself are now fifteen to twenty feet tall, and just beginning to leaf out in the unseasonably warm weather. Water sluices down the passage between the two rows of the still-growing trees. Earlier the stream must have been running much more vigorously given the flattened cattails lying face down in the large pool that serves as an outlet for the creek well up the canyon. The cattails are still alive, with their roots submerged in the pool; the bent plants will no doubt resume their upright posture eventually. Life of all sorts abounds along Deer Creek, much to the pleasure of the very few of us who have come to the stream often enough to document the transformation of the riparian zone and surrounding chaparral following the Willow Fire. It will take years for rebirth of the area to become complete, but even now we can see the power of environmental recovery, a process to be celebrated.

Neon Skimmers

October 2015

The day is warm, sunny, and pleasant, perfect for a walk along Deer Creek. The view from the overlook of the creek bed where the trail first reaches the stream course reveals that the scrub oaks have grown considerably since we first came to this area. The band of small oaks now densely covers a big bend of the creek. And some of the regenerating sycamores are thirty feet tall or thereabouts. But the dead junipers are still dead as a doornail, many still standing, black and grey monuments to the Willow Fire.

Dropping down into the band of oaks by the stream bed, I find a gall growing under an oak leaf, an attractive, dark-banded ball of reddish material inside of which I am guessing that there is (or was) an immature wasp of some sort, perhaps one belonging to the family Cynipidae. The larval wasp, if that was the gall maker, injects chemicals into the plant, which responds to the biochemical manipulation provided by its guest by forming a sphere in which the insect lives and feeds. Is the gall conspicuously colored because the oak manages to make it so, the better to attract consumers such as small birds that will tear the gall open and feed on the insect within? Or is the gall made obvious by the tiny wasp as a way of alerting a would-be predator that the reward for ripping open the colorful gall will be so small as to make the task unprofitable?

On those few occasions when I have tried to find out what was in a leaf gall, I have discovered only a loose network of thin silken (?) lines. Had I been an insectivorous bird, I would have been disappointed as well as educated.

As I walk along, I pass a great many prickly pear cacti decorated with bright red fruits. The adaptive basis of the bright color of these fruits is not a mystery if Daniel Janzen's hypothesis of fruit-eating megafauna is correct. You may remember (see pages 75–76) that he proposed that spiny cactus fruits evolved their conspicuous color to advertise their edibility to very large, hard-mouthed mammals that once roamed the West but are now extinct.

After a couple of hours of ambling slowly upstream, I reach the place where the stream drops down into a small pool largely occupied by cat-tail reeds, a spot where a peanut butter and jelly sandwich can be comfortably consumed. In order to take advantage of this picnic destination, I carefully make my way down to the shelf of dark red rock by the trickling stream and above the much deeper pool. Once there, I remove my sandwich from my backpack and enjoy my small but very edible lunch.

While sitting by the streamlet, I cannot help but notice a large, bright red dragonfly that zips about over the water and sometimes perches on small willows that grow directly out of the stream. Actually there are at least two of these dragonflies (which I later identify as the well-named neon skimmer), with one individual chasing the other in what are surely territorial battles between a resident and an intruder. This is the first time that I have seen this species along Deer Creek, and as is true for so many of the animals here, I will later discover that nothing has ever been reported about the behavior of this fairly common, widespread, and quite beautiful species.

Having studied a few members of the order (the Odonata) to which the neon skimmers belong, I am not surprised to see evidence of aggression between males inasmuch as it is common for odonates to fight with one another in an effort to control a chunk of watery habitat that may be visited by egg-laying females, which are sexually receptive, usually both before and during oviposition. The two males engage in bouts of rapid flight that take them up and down the stream and back again.

Suspecting that the skimmers would not be spending so much time and energy in flying over the stream if there were no females around, I search the tiny channel of the creek for possible females, and soon enough, I discover a female flipping the tip of her abdomen in the water in the manner of many egg-laying odonates. She is a dull tan brown rather than the brilliant red of the male; sexual dimorphism of this sort is another not uncommon feature of dragonflies. But it is odd to me that no male approaches the female even though she continues to lay her eggs in the watercourse that lies within the presumptive territory of a male neon skimmer. Eventually the female finishes her work and flies off into the surrounding vegetation.

Another female arrives near the water and this one is detected quickly by a male (the territorial resident?) that swoops down and grasps the female with his abdominal claspers as a prelude to a quick copulation in the wheel position. The mating is over so quickly that I fail to capture the event with my camera. The female then flies up and perches on a bare branch of a burnt juniper, where she remains for so long that I lose interest in her.

It was already nearly noon when I made my way to the picnic site, and with the passage of time, it is after 1 p.m. when I realize that there are two males perching on the same willow, sometimes within a few inches of one another (figure 59). The mutual tolerance of the two drag-onflies astonishes me since I am quite sure that at least one of the males is a resident territorial individual. I rack my brain for possible expla-nations for this odd behavior. Is male territoriality only worth the time and energy expense before early afternoon? Perhaps females of the neon skimmer search out egg-laying spots early in the day exclusively, and so there are no receptive females left in the early afternoon. Certainly on this day, egg-laying females are scarce when I arrive, and they are absent altogether by 1 p.m. Moreover, perhaps females that have mated earlier are not very receptive later on, which would account for the "failure" of the territorial male to approach and mate with the female that was egg laying presumably in his domain around noontime. I wonder if terri-torial males can identify females with which they have already copu-lated so that these males will then leave their mates alone while they lay

Figure 59. Two male neon skimmer dragonflies perched side by side on the same plant. Why do these territorial males tolerate one another?

their eggs, "knowing" instinctively that females of this sort will not be receptive to them or to another male that happens upon them. My speculations are rampant, testimony to the need for much more research (ideally with marked males and females that have received distinctive paint dots on their thorax), research that would help fill a gap in our knowledge of *Libellula croceipennis*, a species that like so many others has not been studied, judging from the silence of the Web of Science on the biology of this dragonfly.

My guesses about the neon skimmer's mating behavior keep me company on the walk back down to the trailhead. The insects and other animals (to say nothing of the plants) that have returned to Deer Creek after the wildfire could easily entertain the researcher in me for the rest of my life.

Conclusion

The Ecology of Western Wildfires

More than ten years have passed since the Willow Fire incinerated large portions of the Mazatzal Mountains. Over the past decade or so, fire has become widely recognized to be part of the natural scheme of things, with burned forests, chaparral, and grasslands generally recovering after a wildfire. Of course, the time to recovery varies greatly depending on the nature of the plant community and the aridity of the area. In the profoundly dry Mojave and Sonoran Deserts of the Southwest, Scott Abella has assembled data suggesting that a full recovery may take about seventy-five years on average. In wetter chaparral habitats, the time until the plant community is fully restored is considerably shorter, presumably because the plants in these habitats have evolved a tolerance for relatively frequent fires.

But what about the intense fires that take place after a long period of artificial fire suppression by our species or those that occur because of prolonged drought perhaps caused (in part) by anthropogenic global warming? The Willow Fire was a very large and often highly intense fire that burned much of the Mazatzal Mountains, ranging from the lower chaparral of little scrub oaks and other shrubs to the riparian woodland of sycamores and large oak species, and even the forests of pines, including ponderosa at the higher elevations. Ten years after the fire,

Figure 60. Deer Creek and surroundings in October 2014, a few months past the tenth anniversary of the Willow Fire. Although the dead junipers still remain, ten years of recovery has altered the immediate postfire environment a great deal (compare figure 60 with figure 4).

the chaparral at least has regained much of its original character with a dense cover of shrub oaks on the lower slopes (figure 60). True, the junipers have yet to make a start on a comeback, but even so, the hills and valleys around the eastern part of Deer Creek are not all that different than they were ten or eleven years previously, except for the current shortage of junipers.

The Mazatzal chaparral zone has apparently responded in much the same way that California chaparral usually copes with occasional fires. The plants in these areas appear to have evolved in a setting in which fires flare up often enough over time to select for plants that possess roots or seeds that live on after a wildfire. Adaptations of this sort make it possible for a place that has been firebombed to regain its previous dense, vegetative cover in a matter of years, rather than requiring decades or centuries. However, repeated fires with very short intervals between events may be "unnatural" in the sense of producing novel ecological outcomes, as has been suggested for the California chaparral in places near the urban-wildland interface. Here, very frequent fires have produced substantial changes in plant communities in part because the plants that come back during the short intervals between fires may be dominated by exotic aliens rather than by native species. If this outcome occurs, it suggests that the original species found in California chaparral habitats have evolved a capacity to respond to *infrequent* wildfires but not repeated burns over a short period. I hope that the Deer Creek chaparral is not put to the test but can wait a good many years before the next Willow Fire sweeps down the mountainsides to the shrub oak zone.

Unfortunately, the resilience shown by the Mazatzal chaparral is less evident in the riparian zone despite the ability of fast-growing sycamores to sprout from rootstock and the pronounced growth of willows in and along the stream itself. The still incomplete nature of plant recovery is most evident along the stream edge in the general absence of the large evergreen oaks. Here and there, a remnant stand of oaks still exists, trees that were lucky enough to avoid the ravages of the Willow Fire. If recruitment of a new generation of oaks has begun, it has done so in a very subtle and inconspicuous manner.

The stream itself also still shows the effects of having been gouged and scoured by the strong runoffs that occurred after monsoon rains soon after the fire. If the gentle tree-lined brook of the past is to be resurrected, a great many more years will be required, almost certainly far more than I have at my disposal.

The forest that once covered the sides of the canyon carved by Deer Creek in the upper reaches has also been profoundly affected by the Willow Fire. Tall, dead pines leaning off to one side serve as memorials of a sort for their fallen colleagues, the burnt specimens that have toppled over in the last decade. The deeply cut stream and the jumble of fallen logs make it challenging to negotiate the higher portions of Deer Creek, where decades will pass before the forest and stream might regain the tranquil elegance of the past.

Although my amateur's investigation into the postfire recovery of the Mazatzals appears to be the only attempt to document the changes here, fire research is big business in other parts of Arizona. One example is provided by a large team of forest biologists led by Wally Covington at Northern Arizona University. These researchers have begun to establish what works and what does not in the attempt to return the ponderosa pine forests of northern Arizona to something resembling the way these woodlands may have looked before the arrival of Anglo settlers with their cattle and their desire to keep ponderosa pine forests fire-free, especially after 1900.

Covington and his crew believe that the cattle that accompanied pioneer settlers in our state removed the fire-prone grasses from the forests where the beeves grazed. This factor, in addition to the efforts to put out fires quickly, resulted in the widespread growth of "dog hair" stands of densely packed, spindly trees in our mountain forests. Eventually, these stands burned ferociously, unlike the low-intensity, grass-fueled fires in the open ponderosa woodlands of the past. Intense fires not only destroyed young ponderosas but also spread to the crowns of the mature forest trees. These killer conflagrations took out young and old pines alike, requiring very long periods for the forest to reassert itself in anything like its previous form.

If Covington and others who agree with his team are right, we will have to remove cattle from the ponderosa forests *and* chop down the dog hair thickets if we are to reestablish the open, grassy forests of the past. Controlled burns will also be needed to generate the low-intensity wildfires that can sweep through ponderosa pine stands without damaging the really big trees. Thinning is expensive (and controversial if loggers have to be paid for this work by letting them also cut down some economically valuable big boys as well as the nearly worthless little trees). According to Barbara Strom and Peter Fulé, however, thinning does seem to reduce the risk of catastrophic fires and thus to speed recovery of the surviving ponderosas after a fire has occurred.

Nonetheless, it turns out that different patches of ponderosa pine may respond differently to prescribed burns; in one forest, a nonnative brome (cheatgrass) came to predominate after the controlled burn, whereas in another forest, native species did better. Cheatgrass and other aliens are a problem throughout the west because of their ability to exclude the plants that preceded them. If one wants to restore ponderosa pine to presettlement conditions (prior to the unfortunate introduction of cheatgrass), we may have to try to remove or at least reduce the abundance of this grass in pine forests prior to thinning and burning. Ecological restoration is neither cheap nor easy. On the other hand, the complete destruction of mature pine forests by high-intensity crown fires has nasty social, economic, and ecological consequences that should be avoided if at all possible.

I do not know if Covington's prescriptions for pure ponderosa forests are applicable to the mixed-species forests of the Mazatzals. In any event, it seems highly unlikely that the United States Forest Service is going to invest large sums in the ecological restoration of the higher elevation woodlands here. Thank goodness that the lower parts of the mountain range have been able to restore themselves (at least in part and for the moment) with fire-adapted native species leading the way.

I am also unsure whether the climate changes that are taking place throughout the world in general, and western North America in particular, will undo all efforts currently underway to maintain healthy forest ecosystems. The increased spring and summer temperatures of the past several decades, along with a decrease in snowmelt runoff, are thought by some to be the main reasons behind the correlated increase in severe wildfires in the West. These trends seem certain to continue into the future, which is not good news for ponderosa pine forests or the various plant communities that some of us have come to associate with Deer Creek and the Mazatzal Mountains, communities that we and other animals deeply appreciate.

But let's not be entirely negative. The bad news will be here soon enough. For the time being, there is still plenty to enjoy in the recovering chaparral and the growing sycamores and willows in this small part of the world. These plants and others have come back to support a diverse and attractive collection of animals, including assorted insects, birds, and mammals, any one of which can provide a discovery that makes a hike along Deer Creek a pleasure. So get out and take a hike somewhere, anywhere, and perhaps the discoveries that you make will provide you with pleasure and a sense that a natural world persists despite an overabundance of people. I hope so.

Acknowledgments

I have enjoyed my companionship with many fellow hikers when visiting Deer Creek, including my brother Bud, my son Joe, my wife Sue, and a fine botanist, Liz (Elizabeth Makings), among others. Liz provided many useful corrections to the list of scientific names of plants, and she reviewed the entire manuscript, to say nothing of providing identifications of plants on our walks. She also supplied some of the photographs that illustrate the text, as did Evan Rand and Eric Neitzel. Thanks to one and all.

Scientific Names of Plants and Insects

Plants

Babyslippers	*Hybanthus verticillatus*
Barberry	*Berberis fremontii*
Barley, European	*Hordeum vulgare*
Barley, little	*Hordeum pusillum*
Blue dick (or Papago onion)	*Dichelostemma capitatum*
Brome (cheatgrass)	*Bromus tectorum*
Brome, red	*Bromus madritensis rubens*
Camphorweed	*Heterotheca psammophila*
Canyon grape	*Vitis arizonica*
Cactus, barrel	*Ferocactus wislizenii*
Cactus, hedgehog	*Echinocereus* spp.
Cactus, prickly pear	*Opuntia* spp.
Cactus, saguaro	*Carnegiea gigantea*
Cactus, staghorn	*Cylindropuntia acanthocarpa*
Catclaw acacia	*Acacia greggii*
Catclaw mimosa	*Mimosa biuncifera*
Clover, white prairie	*Dalea candida*
Cottonwood	*Populus fremonti*
Deer brush	*Ceanothus integerrimus*

Desert anemone	*Anemone tuberosa*
Desert marigold	*Baileya multiradiata*
Desert paintbrush	*Castilleja chromosa*
Devil's claw	*Proboscidea althaeifolia*
Dodder	*Cuscuta sp.*
Fairy duster	*Calliandra eriophylla*
Four-o'clock, Colorado	*Mirabilis multiflora*
Four-o'clock, scarlet	*Mirabilis coccinea*
Goldenrod	*Solidago sp.*
Goldfields	*Lasthenia californica*
Goodding's verbena	*Verbena gooddingii*
Gordon's bladderpod	*Lesquerella gordonii*
Globemallow	*Sphaeralcea ambigua*
Graham mimosa	*Mimosa biuncifera*
Grass, green sprangletop	*Leptochloa dubia*
Grass, red sprangletop	*Leptochloa panacea* ssp. *brachiata*
Indian paintbrush	*Castilleja sp.*
Juniper	*Juniperus arizonica*
Larkspur, barestem	*Delphinium scaposum*
Lily, winding mariposa	*Calochortus flexuosus*
Locoweed	*Astragalus sp.*
Longflower tubetongue	*Siphonoglossa longiflora*
Longleaf false goldeneye	*Heliomeris longifolia*
Lotus pea	*Lotus sp.*
Lupine, miniature	*Lupinus bicolor*
Lupine, bajada	*Lupinus concinnus*
Lupine, Coulter's	*Lupinus sparsiflorus*
Manzanita, pointleaf	*Arctostaphylos pungens*
Manzanita, Pringle	*Arctostaphylos pringlei*
Mexican poppy	*Eschscholzia mexicana*
Milkweed, antelope horns	*Asclepias asperula*
Milkweed, common	*Asclepias syriaca*
Milkweed, Engelmann's	*Asclepias engelmannii*
Miner's lettuce	*Claytonia perfoliata*

Miniature woollystar	*Eriastrum diffusum*
Morning glory, Arizona blue eyes	*Evolvulus arizonicus*
Morning glory, red star	*Ipomoea coccinea*
Mullein	*Verbascum thapsus*
Nevada biscuitroot	*Lomatium nevadense*
Oak, Emory	*Quercus emoryi*
Oak, shrub live	*Quercus turbinella*
Owl's clover	*Castilleja exserta*
Palo verde, blue	*Parkinsonia florida*
Paperflower	*Psilostrophe cooperi*
Penstemon, Arizona	*Penstemon pseudospectabilis*
Penstemon, Palmer's	*Penstemon palmeri*
Ponderosa pine	*Pinus ponderosa*
Primrose, stemless	*Oenothera caespitosa*
Primrose, Hooker's evening	*Oenothera elata*
Red maids	*Calandrinia ciliata*
Sacred datura	*Datura wrightii*
Salt cedar	*Tamarix ramosissima*
Silk tassel bush	*Garrya flavescens*
Snakeweed, broom	*Gutierrezia sarothrae*
Sotol	*Dasylirion wheeleri*
Storksbill, red-stem	*Erodium cicutarium*
Storksbill, Texas	*Erodium texanum*
Sumac, fragrant	*Rhus aromatica*
Sumac, sugar	*Rhus ovata*
Sweetbush	*Bebbia juncea*
Sycamore	*Platanus wrightii*
Tansyaster, purple	*Machaeranthera sp.*
Twining snapdragon	*Maurandella antirrhinifolia*
White ratany	*Krameria grayi*
Willow	*Salix spp.*
Woollystar	*Eriastrum diffusum*
Yellow blazing star	*Mentzelia jonesii*
Yellow columbine	*Aquilegia chrysantha*

Insects

Ant, harvester	*Pogonomyrmex* spp.
Bee, digger	*Centris pallida*
Beetle, buprestid	*Acmaeodera* spp.
Butterfly, brown elfin	*Callophrys augustinus*
Butterfly, monarch	*Danaus plexippus*
Butterfly, mourning cloak	*Nymphalis antiopa*
Butterfly, Palmer's metalmark	*Apodemia palmeri*
Carpenter bees	*Xylocopa californica, X. tabaniformis,* and *X. varipuncta*
Checkerspot, tiny	*Dymasia dymas*
Crab spider	*Misumena* spp.
Damselfly, great spreadwing	*Archilestes grandis*
Dragonfly, blue-eyed darner	*Aeshna multicolor*
Dragonfly, neon skimmer	*Libellula croceipennis*
Giant agave bug	*Acanthocephala thomasi*
Giant skipper, Arizona	*Agathymus aryxna*
Giant skipper, yucca	*Megathymus yuccae*
Giant water bug	*Abedus herberti*
Grasshopper, green bird	*Schistocerca shoshone*
Grasshopper, oak leaf	*Tomonotus ferruginosus*
Grasshopper, red-shanked	*Xanthippus corallipes*
Grasshopper, red-winged	*Arphia pseudonietana*
Grasshopper, Wheeler's blue-winged	*Leprus wheeleri*
Hawkmoth, five-spotted	*Manduca quinquemaculata*
Hawkmoth, bumblebee	*Hemaris thetis*
Moth, cactus	*Cactoblastis cactorum*
Moth, gaura borer	*Euhagena emphytiformis*
Moth, prickly pear borer	*Melitara dentata*
Moth, underwing	*Catocala* spp.
Sharpshooter, blue-green	*Graphocephala atropunctata*
Soldier beetle	*Chauliognathus lecontei*
Wasp, yellow jacket	*Vespula* sp.
White-skipper, northern	*Heliopetes ericetorum*

Selected Bibliography

Deer Creek Long Ago

On the function of wing colors in underwing moths: Ingalls, V. 1993. Startle and habituation responses of blue jays (*Cyanocitta cristata*) in a laboratory simulation of antipredator defenses of *Catocala* moths (Lepidoptera, Noctuidae). *Behaviour* 126:77–96.

Sargent, T. D. 1973. Studies on the *Catocala* of southern New England. IV. A preliminary analysis of wing-damaged specimens, with discussion of anomaly as a potential antipredator function of hindwing diversity. *Journal of the Lepidopterists' Society* 27:175–192.

Sargent, T. D. 1978. Maintenance of stability in hind-wing diversity among moths of the genus *Catocala* (Lepidotera: Noctuidae). *Evolution* 32:424–434.

Schlenoff, D. H. 1985. The startle responses of blue jays to *Catocala* (Lepidoptera, Noctuidae) prey models. *Animal Behaviour* 33:1057–1067.

The South Fork of Deer Creek: January 2004

Rating of trails at Deer Creek: http://hikearizona.com/decoder.php?ZTN=35.

The Willow Fire and Its Aftermath: June 2004 and April 2005

A list of Arizona's biggest wildfires: https://en.wikipedia.org/wiki/List_of_Arizona_wildfires.

Peppin, D. L., P. Z. Fulé, C. H. Sieg, J. L. Beyers, and M. E. Hunter. 2010. Post-wildfire seeding in forests of the western United States: An evidence-based review. *Forest Ecology and Management* 260:573–586.

Peppin, D. L., P. Z. Fulé, C. H. Sieg, J. L. Beyers, M. E. Hunter, and P. R. Robichaud. 2011. Recent trends in post-wildfire seeding in western US forests: costs and seed mixes. *International Journal of Wildland Fire* 20:702–708.

Kuenzi, A. F., P. Z. Fulé, and C. H. Sieg. 2007. Effects of fire severity and pre-stand treatment on community recovery after a large wildfire. *Forest Ecology and Management* 255:855–865.

Returning to Deer Creek: December 2008

On the creation of the Agua Fria National Monument: http://www.blm.gov/style/medialib/blm/az/images/afria.Par.42965.File.dat/Stone_AAC_Prescott_06.pdf.

Spring Revival: May 2009

The genus *Mirabilis* as covered in *Wikipedia*: http://en.wikipedia.org/wiki/Mirabilis_%28plant%29.

On hawkmoths as specialized flower pollinators: http://www.fs.fed.us/wildflowers/pollinators/pollinator-of-the-month/hawk_moths.shtml.

More on hawkmoth behavior and pollination: Raguso, R. A., and M. A. Willis. 2003. Hawkmoth pollination in Arizona's Sonoran Desert: Behavioral responses to floral traits. In *Butterflies: Ecology and Evolution Taking Flight*, eds. C. L. Boggs, W. B. Watts, and P. R. Ehrlich. University of Chicago Press, Chicago.

On the ability of hawkmoths to use humidity around flowers to determine the amount of nectar in a flower: von Arx, M., J. Goyret, G. Davidowitz, and R. A. Raguso. 2012. Floral humidity as a reliable sensory cue for profitability assessment by nectar-foraging hawkmoths. *Proceedings of the National Academy of Sciences* 109:9471–9476.

Walker-Larsen, J., and L. D. Harder. 2001. Vestigial organs as opportunities for functional innovation: The example of the *Penstemon* staminode. *Evolution* 55:477–487.

After the Monsoon: September 2009

A paper on the variety of signals provided by plants like Hooker's evening primrose to attract pollinators in the evening and at night: Baker, H. G. 1961. Adaptation of flowering plants to nocturnal and crepuscular pollinators. *Quarterly Review of Biology* 36:64–73.

Hooker's evening primrose attracts large bees in addition to hawkmoth pollinators: Barthell, J. F., and J. M. H. Knops. 1997. Visitation of evening primrose by carpenter bees: Evidence of a "mixed" pollination syndrome. *Southwestern Naturalist* 42:86–93.

The green lynx spider is the subject of a report in BugGuide.net: http://bugguide.net/node/view/2032.

The Lupine Season: March 2010

Evidence that the invasive storksbill arrived in California before the Spanish and their cattle: Mensing, S., and R. Byrne. 1998. Pre-mission invasion of *Erodium cicutarium* in California. *Journal of Biogeography* 25:757–762.

How storksbill disperses its seeds: Evangelista, D., S. Hotton, and J. Dumais. 2011. The mechanics of explosive dispersal and self-burial in the seeds of the filaree, *Erodium cicutarium* (Geraniaceae). *Journal of Experimental Biology* 214:521–529.

Edible plants: http://honest-food.net/2011/02/23/on-miners-lettuce-americas -gift-to-salad/.

Spring on Deer Creek: Early April 2010

The factors involved in the severe declines and extinctions of many frogs and other amphibians: Collins, J. P., and M. L. Crump. 2009. *Extinction in Our Times: Global Amphibian Decline.* Oxford University Press, New York.

The evolutionary relationships among populations of the canyon treefrog: Barber, P. H. 1999. Phylogeography of the canyon treefrog *Hyla arenicolor* (Cope), based on mitochondrial DNA sequence data. *Molecular Ecology* 8:547–562.

On the disadvantages of additional population growth: Mill, J. S. 1844. *Essays on Some Unsettled Questions of Political Economy.* John W. Parker, London.

Hall, C. S. A., and J. Day. 2014. Why aren't contemporary ecologists and economists addressing resource and energy scarcity: the major problems of the 21st century? *Ecological Engineering* 65:49–53.

Future population growth estimates: https://en.wikipedia.org/wiki/Projections_ of_population_growth.

Dodder and Hedgehogs: Late April 2010

Dodder behavior and the chemical defenses of a host plant: Kelly, C. K. 1992. Resource choice in *Cuscuta europaea. Proceedings of the National Academy of Sciences* 89:12194–12197.

Runyon, J. B., M. C. Mescher, G. W. Felton, and C. M. De Moraes. 2010. Parasitism by *Cuscuta pentagona* sequentially induces JA and SA defence pathways in tomato. *Plant Cell and Environment* 33:290–303.

Disturbance actually helps at least one hedgehog cactus: Martorell, C., P. P. Garcillan, and F. Casillas. 2012. Ruderality in extreme-desert cacti? Population effects of chronic anthropogenic disturbance on *Echinocereus lindsayi. Population Ecology* 54:335–346.

On the distance that a hedgehog cactus might have to travel to cope with climate change: Butler, C. J., E. A. Wheeler, and L. B. Stabler. 2012. Distribution of the threatened lace hedgehog cactus (*Echinocereus reichenbachii*) under various climate change scenarios. *Journal of the Torrey Botanical Society* 139:46–55.

Golden Eagles: Early June 2010

On the reclassification of the twining snapdragon: Albach, D. C., H. M. Meudt, and B. Oxelman. 2005. Piecing together the "new" Plantaginaceae. *American Journal of Botany* 92:297–315.

On the toxic leaves of *Maurandella* and the ability of certain insects to make use of these protected leaves: Dobler, S., G. Petschenka, and H. Pankoke. 2011. Coping with toxic plant compounds: The insect's perspective on iridoid glycosides and cardenolides. *Phytochemistry* 72:1593–1604.

More on the relationship between toxic plants and insect consumers: Opitz, S. E. W., and C. Müller. 2009. Plant chemistry and insect sequestration. *Chemoecology* 19:117–154.

The variable palatability of milkweeds and their use by monarch butterflies: Brower, L. P. 1969. Ecological chemistry. *Scientific American* 220(2):22–29.

On the presence of toxins in a milkweed used by caterpillars of the monarch butterfly: Martin, R. A., and S. P. Lynch. 1988. Cardenolide content and thin-layer chromatography profiles of monarch butterflies, *Danaus plexippus* L. (Lepidoptera, Danaidae) and their larval host-plant milkweed, *Asclepias asperula* subsp. *capricornu* (Woods) (Apocynales, Asclepiadaceae) in north central Texas. *Journal of Chemical Ecology* 14:295–318.

How some insects counteract the gluey defense system of milkweeds: Dussourd, D. E., and T. Eisner. 1987. Vein-cutting behavior: Insect counterploy to the latex defense of plants. *Science* 237:898–901.

On why monarch populations are in trouble: Brower, L. P., O. R. Taylor, E. H. Williams, D. A. Slayback, R. R. Zubieta, and M. I. Ramirez. 2012. Decline of monarch butterflies overwintering in Mexico: is the migratory phenomenon at risk? *Insect Conservation and Diversity* 5:95–100.

Great Spreadwings: October 2010

On the behavior of the great spreadwing damselfly: Bick, G. H., and J. C. Bick. 1970. Oviposition in *Archilestes grandis* (Rambur) (Odonata: Lesidae). *Entomological News* 81:157–163.

On the antipredator value of disruptive coloration: Diamond, J., and A. B. Bond. 2013. The visual trickery of obscured animals. *American Scientist* 102:52–59.

The Puzzle of Dioecy: January 2011

Darwin's explanations for dioecy: Darwin, C. 1877. *The Different Forms of Flowers on the Plants of the Same Species.* John Murray, London.

On the significance of the kind of pollinator on the evolution of dioecy: Borkent, C. J., and L. D. Harder. 2007. Flies (Diptera) as pollinators of two dioecious plants: behaviour and implications for plant mating. *Canadian Entomologist* 139:235–246.

How male and female individuals of certain plants occupy different habitats: Cox, P. A. 1981. Niche partitioning between sexes of dioecious plants. *American Naturalist* 117:295–307.

An article on the Internet on the supposed medicinal benefits of *Garrya* leaves: http://www.naturalwellbeing.com/learning-center/wiki/garrya_leaf/.

Deer Brush and Recovery After Fire: April 2011

A governmental publication that claims that deer brush does better after a fire than before thanks to the ability of its seeds to survive wildfire and the ability of its roots to fix nitrogen: http://pubs.usgs.gov/fs/2011/3140/.

Mites, Glochids, and Thunderstorms: July 2011

A natural history of a mite: Tevis, L., and I. M. Newell. 1962. Studies on biology and seasonal cycle of giant red velvet mite, *Dinothrombium pandorae* (Acari, Trombidiidae). *Ecology* 43:497–505.

More information about and photos of *Dinothrombium* velvet mites: http://www.birdandhike.com/Wildlife/Invert/Ph_Arthropoda/SubP_Chelicerata/Cl_Arachnida/O_Acarina/Acari/Trombid/_Dinothrom.htm.

The hypothesis that many plants produce fruits that evolved to attract now-extinct large mammals: Janzen, D. H., and P. S. Martin. 1982. Neotropical anachronisms: The fruits the gomphotheres ate. *Science* 215:19–27.

Stone, E. C., and G. Juhren. 1951. The effect of fire on the germination of the seeds of *Rhus ovata* Wats. *American Journal of Botany* 38:368–372.

A Day Full of Predators: September 2011

A paper documenting the relatively short life of male tarantulas versus females: Perez-Miles, F., R. Postiglioni, L. Montes de Oca, L. Baruffaldi, and F. G. Costa. 2007. Mating system in the tarantula spider *Eupalaestrus weijenberghi* (Thorell, 1894): Evidences of monandry and polygyny. *Zoology* 11:253–260.

How cannibalistic female spiders benefit from killing and eating males that they capture: Rabaneda-Bueno, R., M. Á. Rodríguez-Gironés, S. Aguado de la Paz, C. Fernández-Montraveta, E. De Mas, D.H. Wise, and J. Moya-Laraño. 2008. Sexual cannibalism: High incidence in a natural population with benefits for females. *PloS One* DOI: 10.1371/journal.pone.0003484.

Three views on why some male arthropods might die at the "hands" of a cannibalistic mate: Gould, S. J. 1984. Only his wings remained. *Natural History* 93:10–18; versus Andrade, M. C. B. 1996. Sexual selection for male sacrifice in the Australian redback spider. *Science* 271:70–72. Also: Berning, A. W., R. D. H. Gadd, K. Sweeney, L. MacDonald, R. Y. Y. Eng, Z. L. Hess, and J. N. Pruitt. 2012. Sexual cannibalism is associated with female behavioural type, hunger state and increased hatching success. *Animal Behaviour* 84: 715–721.

Two papers testing the proposition that male mantids attempt to reduce the risk of sexual cannibalism when interacting with females: Maxwell, M. R., K. M. Gallego, and K. L. Barry. 2010. Effects of female feeding regime in a sexually cannibalistic mantid: fecundity, cannibalism, and male response in *Stagmomantis limbata* (Mantodea). *Ecological Entomology* 35:775–787.

Lelito, J. P., and W. D. Brown. 2008. Mate attraction by females in a sexually cannibalistic praying mantis. *Behavioral Ecology and Sociobiology* 63:313–320.

Male mantids can tell the difference between protein-fed and lipid-fed females: Barry, K. L., and S. M. Wilder. 2013. Macronutrient intake affects reproduction in a predatory insect. *Oikos* 122:1058–1064.

Evidence from an ancient fossilized soldier beetle that chemical secretions were part of its defense system: Poinar, G. O., C. J. Marshall, and R. Buckley. 2007. One hundred million years of chemical warfare by insects. *Journal of Chemical Ecology* 33:1663–1669.

Daddy Water Bugs: November 2011

On the behavior of male water bugs: Smith, R. L. 1979. Repeated copulation and sperm precedence: Paternity assurance for a male brooding water bug. *Science* 205:1029–1031.

Smith, R. L. 1979. Paternity assurance and altered roles in the mating behavior of a giant water bug *Abedus herberti* (Heteroptera: Belostomatidae). *Animal Behaviour* 27:716–728.

Smith, R. L. 1997. Evolution of paternal care in giant water bugs (Heteroptera: Belostomatidae). In *Social Competition and Cooperation Among Insects and Arachnids, II. Evolution of Sociality*, eds. J. C. Choe and B. J. Crespi. Cambridge University Press, Cambridge.

Sperm competition and male praying mantis adaptations: Allen, L. E., K. L. Barry, G. I. Holwell, and M. E. Herberstein. 2011. Perceived risk of sperm competition affects juvenile development and ejaculate expenditure in male praying mantids. *Animal Behaviour* 82:1201–1206.

Mountaintop Snow: December 2011

Heinrich, B. 2003. Overnighting of golden-crowned kinglets in winter. *Wilson Bulletin* 115:113–114.

On the multiple effects of climate change to streams in the American West as a result of altered snowmelt regimes: Perry, L. G., D. C. Anderson, L. V. Reynolds, S. M. Nelson, and P. B. Shafroth. 2012. Vulnerability of riparian ecosystems to elevated CO_2 and climate change in arid and semiarid western North America. *Global Change Biology* 18:821–842.

The International Panel on Climate Change, 2007 report: https://www.ipcc.ch/publications_and_data/publications_ipcc_fourth_assessment_report_synthesis_report.htm.

Pew Research Center report on American attitudes toward global warming: http://www.pewglobal.org/2015/11/05/global-concern-about-climate-change-broad-support-for-limiting-emissions/.

Another report on American attitudes toward global warming: https://www.washingtonpost.com/news/the-fix/wp/2013/04/22/how-americans-see-global-warming-in-8-charts/.

Plass's original article on carbon dioxide's effect on the climate and two commentaries on this classic paper: Plass, G. N., J. R. Fleming, and G. Schmidt. 2010. Carbon dioxide and the climate. *American Scientist* 98:58–67.

Ralph Keeling discusses the significance of his father's measurements of carbon dioxide in the atmosphere over Mauna Loa, Hawaii: Keeling, R. F. 2008. Recording Earth's vital signs. *Science* 319:1771–1772.

"Spring" Is Here: January 2012

On the adaptations to wildfire by *Arctostaphylos* shrubs: Jurado, E., M. Marquez-Linares, and J. Flores. 2011. Effect of cold storage, heat, smoke and charcoal on breaking seed dormancy of *Arctostaphylos pungens* HBK (Ericaceae). *Phyton* 80:101–105.

Overby, S. T., and H. M. Perry. 1996. Direct effects of prescribed fire on available nitrogen and phosphorus in an Arizona chaparral watershed. *Arid Soil Research and Rehabilitation* 10:347–357.

The Creek Is Running: February 2012

Among the forbs examined here is *Lomatium nevadense*: Wrobleski, D. W., and J. B. Kaufmann. 2003. Initial effects of prescribed fire on morphology, abundance, and phenology of forbs in big sagebrush communities in southeastern Oregon. *Restoration Ecology* 11:82–90.

On extrafloral nectaries: Bentley, B. 1976. Plants bearing extrafloral nectaries and associated ant community: Interhabitat differences in reduction of herbivore damage. *Ecology* 57:815–820.

Ness, J. H., W. F. Morris, and J. L. Bronstein. 2009. For ant-protected plants, the best defense is a hungry offense. *Ecology* 90:2823–2831.

So Much for Spring: April 2012

Delphinium spurs: Jabbour, F., and S. S. Renner. 2012. Spurs within spurs: Perianth evolution in the Delphiniaea (Ranunculaceae). *International Journal of Plant Science* 173:1036–1054.

On Augustus, the heroic Inuit, in the *Canadian Encyclopedia*: http://www.the canadianencyclopedia.com/en/article/augustus/.

Megathymus in Florida: Trager, M. D., B. M. Boyd, J. C. Daniels, and J. A. Pence. 2009. Host plant selection, larval survival, and reproductive phenology in *Megathymus yuccae* (Lepidoptera: Hesperiidae). *Environmental Entomology* 38:1211–1218.

Why mourning cloak larvae feed in groups: Tinbergen, N. 1958. *Curious Naturalists*. Basic Books, New York.

An Illegal Hike?: July 2012

The history of elk in Arizona (by Arizona Game and Fish): https://www.azgfd .com/hunting/species/biggame/elk.

Black-necked garter snake natural history: http://www.reptilesofaz.org/Snakes -Subpages/h-t-cyrtopsis.html.

Another Illegal Hike?: August 2012

For information about devil's claw in Arizona, see SEINet: http://swbiodiversity. org/seinet/taxa/index.php?taxon=1487.

The foraging behavior of *Schistocerca shoshone*: Chambers, P., G. Sword, J. E. Angel, S. Behmer, and A. E. Bernays. 1996. Foraging by generalist grasshoppers: Two different strategies. *Animal Behaviour* 52:155–165.

Sprangletop Heaven: September 2012

Basic data on red or mucronate sprangletop grass: http://www.iucnredlist.org/ details/164493/0.

Broussalis, A. M., S. Clemente, and G. E. Ferraro. 2010. *Hybanthus parviflorus* (Violaceae): Insecticidal activity of a South American plant. *Crop Protection* 29:953–956.

Fall in Deer Creek: October 2012

On the biological control of an invasive plant: Freeman, D. B. 1992. Prickly pear menace in eastern Australia 1880–1940. *Geographical Review* 82: 413–428.

An article on the adaptive value of red leaves for plants in the fall: Guy, Robert D., and J. Krakowski. 2003. Autumn colours—nature's canvas is a silk parasol. *Davidsonia* 14(4):111–120.

A report from a conference on the adaptive value of red leaves for plants in the fall: http://onlinelibrary.wiley.com/doi/10.1111/j.1469-8137.2008.02505 .x/full.

Archetti, M., et al. 2009. Unravelling the evolution of autumn colours: an interdisciplinary approach. *Trends in Ecology & Evolution* 24:166–173.

The Cold Carpenter Bee: December 2012

Two papers on the mating system of the valley carpenter bee: Marshall, L. D., and J. Alcock. 1981. The evolution of the mating system of the carpenter bee *Xylocopa varipuncta* (Hymenoptera: Anthophoridae). *Journal of Zoology* 193:315–324.

Alcock, J., and A. P. Smith. 1987. Hilltopping, leks and female choice in the carpenter bee *Xylocopa* (*Neoxylocopa*) *varipuncta*. *Journal of Zoology* 211:1–10.

Two papers on the mating system(s) of the mountain carpenter bee: Janzen, D. H. 1964. Notes on the behavior of four subspecies of the carpenter bee, *Xylocopa* (*Notoxylocopa*) *tabaniformis*, in Mexico. *Annals of the Entomological Society of America* 57:296–301.

O'Brien, L. B., and P. D. Hurd. 1965. Carpenter bees of the subgenus *Notoxylocopa* (Hymenoptera: Apoidea). *Annals of the Entomological Society of America* 58:175–196.

On the chemical defenses of coreid bugs and their relatives: Aldrich, J. R. 1988. Chemical ecology of the Heteroptera. *Annual Review of Entomology* 33:211–238.

Wasp mimicry documented in flying buprestid beetles: Silberglied, R. E., and T. Eisner. 1969. Mimicry of beetles with unconventional flight. *Science* 163:486–488.

The Leafhopper Walk: January 2013

de Groot, M., M. Derlink, P. Pavlovcic, J. Presern, A. Cokl, and M. Virant-Doberlet. 2012. Duetting behaviour in the leafhopper *Aphrodes makarovi* (Hemiptera: Cicadellidae). *Journal of Insect Behavior* 25:419–440.

Eriksson, A., G. Anfora, A. Lucchi, F. Lanzo, M. Virant-Doberlet, and V. Mazzoni. 2012. Exploitation of insect vibrational signals reveals a new method of pest management. *PloS One* 7:5 e32954 DOI: 10.1371/journal.pone.0032954.

Mazzoni, V., J. Presern, A. Lucchi, and M. Virant-Doberlet. 2009. Reproductive strategy of the Nearctic leafhopper *Scaphoideus titanus* Ball (Hemiptera: Cicadellidae). *Bulletin of Entomological Research* 99:401–413.

Percy, D. M., E. A. Boyd, and M. S. Hoddle. 2008. Observations of acoustic signaling in three sharpshooters: *Homalodisca vitripennis*, *Homalodisca liturata*, and *Graphocephala atropunctata* (Hemiptera: Cicadellidae). *Annals of the Entomological Society of America* 101:253–259.

Virant-Doberlet, M., R. A. King, J. Polajnar, and W. O. C. Symondson. 2011. Molecular diagnostics reveal spiders that exploit prey vibrational signals used in sexual communication. *Molecular Ecology* 20:2204–2216.

The Coyote Chorus: February 2013

Lehner, P. N. 1978. Coyote vocalizations: a lexicon and comparisons with other species. *Animal Behaviour* 26:712–722.

Bekoff, M., and M. C. Well. 1986. Social ecology and behavior of coyotes. *Advances in the Study of Behavior* 16:251–338.

Petroelje, T. R., J. L. Belant, and D. E. Beyer, Jr. 2013. Factors affecting the elicitation of vocal responses from coyotes *Canis latrans*. *Wildlife Biology* 19:41–47.

Another Spring: March 2013

Information on locoweed (*Astragalus*): https://en.wikipedia.org/wiki/Astragalus.

Back to Deer Creek: October 2013

The possible functions of white outer tail feathers in birds: Jablonski, P. G. 2001. Sensory exploitation of prey: manipulation of the initial direction of prey escapes by a conspicuous "rare enemy." *Proceedings of the Royal Society B* 268:1017–1022.

De L. Brooke, M. 2010. Unexplained recurrent features of the plumage of birds. *Ibis* 152:845–847.

Hill, J. A., D. A. Enstrom, E. D. Ketterson, V. Nolan, Jr., and C. Ziegenfus. 1999. Mate choice based on static versus dynamic secondary sexual traits in the dark-eyed junco. *Behavioral Ecology* 10:91–96.

An image collection of *Euhagena* moths: http://mothphotographersgroup. msstate.edu/species.php?hodges=2534.

On the possible nutritional value of cannibalism: Meffe, G. K., and M. L. Crump. 1987. Possible growth and reproductive benefits of cannibalism in the mosquitofish. *American Naturalist* 129:203–212; versus Wilder, S. M., and A. L. Rypstra. 2010. Males make poor meals: a comparison of nutrient extraction during sexual cannibalism and predation. *Oecologia* 162:617–625.

Winter, Arizona Style: December 2013

Problems associated with invasive exotics: Keane, R. M., and M. J. Crawley. 2002. Exotic plant invasions and the enemy release hypothesis. *Trends in Ecology & Evolution* 17:164–170.

Stein, B., L. S. Kutner, and J. S. Adams. 2000. *Precious Heritage: The Status of Biodiversity in the United States*. Oxford University Press, Oxford.

An invasive plant that may have been unfairly labeled a pest species: Stromberg, J. C., M. K. Chew, P. L. Nagler, and E. P. Glenn. 2009. Changing perceptions of change: the role of scientists in *Tamarix* and river management. *Restoration Ecology* 17:177–186.

The cause of size differences between males and females: Alcock, J., C. E. Jones, and S. L. Buchmann. 1977. Male mating strategies in the bee *Centris pallida* Fox (Hymenoptera: Anthophoridae). *American Naturalist* 111:145–155.

Stubblefield, J. W., and J. Seger. 1994. Sexual dimorphism in the Hymenoptera. In *Differences Between the Sexes*, eds. R. V. Short and E. Balaban. Cambridge University Press, Cambridge.

Robins in Winter: February 2014

Overwintering butterflies are affected by climate change: Diamond, S. E., A. M. Frame, R. A. Martin, and L. B. Buckley. 2011. Species' traits predict phenological responses to climate change in butterflies. *Ecology* 92:1005–1012.

Yet Another Spring: March 2014

On why harvester ants remove the plants growing above their underground nests: Bucy, A. M., and M. D. Breed. 2006. Thermoregulatory trade-offs result from vegetation removal by a harvester ant. *Ecological Entomology* 31:423–429.

On the effects of seed disposal around the nest disks of harvester ants: Mac-Mahon, J. A., J. F. Mull, and T. O. Crist. 2000. Harvester ants (*Pogonomyrmex* spp.): Their community and ecosystem influences. *Annual Review of Ecology and Systematics* 31:265–291.

Boulton, A. M., and K. D. Amberman. 2006. How ants increase soil biota richness and abundance: a field experiment. *Biodiversity and Conservation* 15:69–82.

On *Hordeum pusillum*, the little barley: https://en.wikipedia.org/wiki/Hordeum_pusillum.

Plant Colors and Plant Visitors: April 2014

On insect color vision: Von Frisch, K. 1956. *Bees: Their Vision, Chemical Senses and Language.* Cornell University Press, Ithaca, NY.

On insect vision and flower colors: Chittka, L., and R. Menzel. 1992. The evolutionary adaptation of flower colour and the insect pollinators' colour vision. *Journal of Comparative Physiology A* 171:171–181.

Menzel, R., and A. Shmida. 1993. The ecology of flower colours and the natural colour vision of insect pollinators: The Israeli flora as a study case. *Biological Reviews* 68:81–120.

The flower color red and its association with bird pollinators: Rodríguez-Gironés, M. A., and L. Santamaría. 2004. Why are so many bird flowers red? *PloS Biology* 2: DOI: 10.1371/journal.pbio.0020350.

On the use of fruit color by birds: Schaefer, H. M., D. J. Levey, V. Schaefer, and M. L. Schaefer. 2006. The role of chromatic and achromatic signals for fruit detection by birds. *Behavioral Ecology* 17:784–789.

Schaefer, H. M., K. McGraw, and C. Catoni. 2008. Birds use fruit color as honest signal of antioxidant rewards. *Functional Ecology* 22:303–310.

Flower color changes as an adaptation for both plants and pollinators: Weiss, M. R. 1991. Floral color changes as cues for pollinators. *Nature* 354:227–229.

Why do young leaves of some plants look red instead of green? Queensborough, S. A., M. R. Metz, R. Valencia, and S. J. Wright. 2013. Demographic consequences of chromatic leaf defence in tropical tree communities: do red young leaves increase growth and survival? *Annals of Botany* 112:677–684.

Back to Deer Creek Again: October 2014

Arizonan monarch butterfly migration patterns: http://www.swmonarchs.org/ (Southwest Monarch Study).

Eastern monarch population issues: http://www.monarchwatch.org/ (Monarch Watch).

Petitioning the federal government about the declining monarch population: http://www.biologicaldiversity.org/news/press_releases/2014/monarch-butterfly-08-26-2014.html.

See also: http://www.xerces.org/wp-content/uploads/2014/08/monarch-esa
-petition.pdf.

Crab Spiders: March 2015

A sampler of papers on the various hypotheses pertaining to the adaptive value
of crab spider coloration: Brechbuhl, R., J. Casas, and S. Bacher. 2010. Inef-
fective crypsis in a crab spider: a prey community perspective. *Proceedings
of the Royal Society B* 277:739–746.

Gawryszewski, F. M., A. L. Llandres, and M. E. Herberstein. 2012. Relationship
between colouration and body condition in a crab spider that lures pollinators. *Journal of Experimental Biology* 215:1128–1136.

Heiling, A. M., M. E. Herberstein, and L. Chittka. 2003. Crab-spiders manipulate flower signals. *Nature* 421:334.

Jones, E. I., and A. Dornhaus. 2011. Predation risk makes bees reject rewarding
flowers and reduce foraging activity. *Behavioral Ecology and Sociobiology*
65:1505–1511.

Llandres, A. L., and M. A. Rodríguez-Gironés. 2011. Movement, UV reflectance
and size, but not spider crypsis, affect the response of honeybees to Australian crab spiders. *PloS One* 6: DOI: 10.1371/journal.pone.0017136.

Llandres, A. L., F. Figon, J. P. Christides, N. Mandon, and J. Casas. 2013. Environmental and hormonal factors controlling reversible colour change in
crab spiders. *Journal of Experimental Biology* 216:3886–3895.

Neon Skimmers: October 2015

On territoriality by male dragonflies in relation to their reproductive activity:
Koenig, W. D., and S. S. Albano. 1985. Patterns of territoriality and mating
success in the white-tailed skimmer *Plathemis lydia* (Odonata: Anisoptera).
American Midland Naturalist 114:1–12.

Marden, J. H., and J. R. Cobb. 2004. Territorial and mating success of dragonflies that vary in muscle power output and presence of gregarine gut parasites. *Animal Behavior* 68:857–865.

Pezella, V. M. 1979. Behavioral ecology of the dragonfly *Libellula pulchella*
Drury (Odonata: Anisoptera). *American Midland Naturalist* 102:1–22.

Conclusion: The Ecology of Western Wildfires

Abella, S. R. 2010. Disturbance and plant success in the Mojave and Sonoran
Deserts of the American Southwest. *International Journal of Environmental
Research and Public Health* 7:1248–1284.

Beschta, R. L., J. J. Rhodes, J. B. Kauffman, R. E. Griesswell, G. W. Minshall, J. R. Karr, D. A. Perry, E. R. Hauer, and C. A. Frissell. 2004. Postfire management on forested public lands of the western United States. *Conservation Biology* 18:957–967.

Dodson, E. K., D. W. Peterson, and R. J. Harrod. 2010. Impacts of erosion control treatments on native vegetation recovery after severe wildfire in the Eastern Cascades, USA. *International Journal of Wildland Fire* 19:490–499.

Keeley, J. E., and T. J. Brennan. 2012. Fire-driven alien invasion in a fire-adapted ecosystem. *Oecologia* 169:1043–1052.

Lipitt, C. L., D. A. Stow, J. F. O'Leary, and J. Franklin. 2013. Influence of short-interval fire occurrence and post-fire recovery of fire-prone shrublands in California, USA. *International Journal of Wildland Fire* 22:184–193.

Malakoff, D. 2002. Arizona ecologist puts stamp on forest restoration debate. *Science* 297:2194–2196.

Strom, B. A., and P. Z. Fulé. 2007. Pre-wildfire fuel treatments affect long-term ponderosa pine forest dynamics. *International Journal of Wildland Fire* 16:128–138.

Suding, K. N. 2011. Toward an era of restoration in ecology: Successes, failures, and opportunities ahead. *Annual Review of Ecology, Evolution, and Systematics* 42:465–487.

Swetnam, T. W., C. D. Allen, and J. L. Betancourt. 1999. Applied historical ecology: Using the past to manage for the future. *Ecological Applications* 9:1189–1206.

Westerling, A. L., H. G. Hidalgo, D. R. Cayan, and T. W. Swetnam. 2007. Warming and earlier spring increase western US forest wildfire activity. *Science* 313:940–943.

Index

About the Author

John Alcock is an Emeritus Regent's Professor in the School of Life Sciences at Arizona State University, where he taught from 1973 until 2008. He is the author of a number of books on the natural history of the Sonoran Desert, notably *Sonoran Desert Spring* and *Sonoran Desert Summer* (published by the University of Arizona Press), as well as a textbook on animal behavior, his teaching specialty. His personal research, which still continues, focuses on the mating behavior of insects, a branch of natural history that has provided him with subjects ranging from bees to wasps to flies and beyond. In addition to enjoying watching insects and learning about their lives, he is a hiker and photographer. He has been married to Sue Alcock for almost fifty years, and they have two sons, one a lawyer in Phoenix, Arizona, and the other a doctor in Albuquerque, New Mexico.